No
Worries

No Worries

HOW TO LIVE
A STRESS-FREE
FINANCIAL LIFE

Jared
Dillian

Harriman
House

HARRIMAN HOUSE LTD
3 Viceroy Court
Bedford Road
Petersfield
Hampshire
GU32 3LJ
GREAT BRITAIN
Tel: +44 (0)1730 233870

Email: enquiries@harriman-house.com
Website: harriman.house

First published in 2023.
Copyright © Jared Dillian

The right of Jared Dillian to be identified as the Author has been asserted in accordance with the Copyright, Design and Patents Act 1988.

Hardback ISBN: 978-1-80409-040-4
Paperback ISBN: 978-1-80409-055-8
eBook ISBN: 978-1-80409-041-1

British Library Cataloguing in Publication Data
A CIP catalogue record for this book can be obtained from the British Library.

Whilst every effort has been made to ensure that information in this book is accurate, no liability can be accepted for any loss incurred in any way whatsoever by any person relying solely on the information contained herein.

No responsibility for loss occasioned to any person or corporate body acting or refraining to act as a result of reading material in this book can be accepted by the Publisher, by the Author, or by the employers of the Author.

The Publisher does not have any control over or any responsibility for any Author's or third-party websites referred to in or on this book.

CONTENTS

....

INTRODUCTION

....

I have some money now, but that was not always the case.

And yet, apart from two brief moments, I have lived a stress-free financial life. It has increased my happiness a hundredfold.

I am the offspring of a Coast Guard helicopter pilot and a schoolteacher. After my parents' divorce, I grew up in southeastern Connecticut, raised by my mother and my grandmother. My grandmother passed away when I was 14. During my childhood, we didn't have much—we weren't poor, but at the time we were considered lower-middle class.

I have very distinct memories of something approaching hardship from my childhood. We got some, but not all, of my clothes from yard sales. I had one blue and purple jacket that I wore throughout the winter, and I had that jacket for years. I was on the borderline of getting free lunch at school. We had an old wooden TV set with a rotor that spun the antenna on the roof.

In spite of not having a lot, Christmas was never an issue—I would dutifully write out my list for Santa and most of it would end up under the tree. We also had a small amount of alimony from my grandmother's divorce.

But there were no extravagances. If we took a vacation, it was by car. We took one summer vacation to New Hampshire where I was astounded that we were paying $90 a night for a hotel room. That is the biggest luxury that I can remember from those days. Like I said, though, we weren't poor, and my mom did the best she could with what she had.

Fast forward to today. I made $1.7 million last year in business income, not including investment gains.

Now, this is not a book about how to get rich. There are plenty of those books out there, varying in quality. Along the way, we will talk a little bit about how to get rich, but that is not the focus of this book.

The focus of *No Worries* is how to minimize your financial *stress*.

Millions of people experience crippling financial stress. They lay awake at night, wondering how they're going to pay the rent. They make payments on their student loans for years, then find that the loan balance is significantly larger than when they started. They buy some stupid stock and set fire to a bunch of money, and yet they hold on, hoping that it will come back.

Financial stress compounds other kinds of stress: marriages, jobs, kids. It makes your life difficult.

The thing about money stress is that it's *unnecessary*. It is possible to live a stress-free financial life.

Most people believe that the antidote to financial stress is more money. But it's not. A stress-free financial life is a function of how you structure your financial affairs, and your attitudes toward money. In this book, we will talk about both.

There is a fallacy in the personal finance discipline that having money is the product of a million small daily decisions. As it turns out, if you get the big decisions right, then you don't have to worry about the small decisions. That's it. If you get the house right, the car right, the student loans right, and set up a simple, diversified investment portfolio, chances are you won't have to worry about giving up coffee. If you're stressed out, you're doing it wrong.

At this point you're likely asking, "How DO I get the big decisions right?" In the pages ahead, we'll break it down by examining the only two sources of financial stress: debt and risk.

....

I live in Myrtle Beach, South Carolina. I moved here from New York City 13 years ago. While I was in New York City, I talked to hedge fund managers and investment bankers. In Myrtle Beach, I have talked to roofers, hospitality workers, and painters.

What I started to learn was that the people of New York and the people of Myrtle Beach had a lot in common. They all worried about money. And they had the exact same money worries: they worried about debt, and they worried about risk.

Debt and risk are the two sources of financial stress—there are no others.

Debt stress can occur when you buy a house, buy a car, go to school, or use credit cards. Risk stress can occur when you invest.

Avoid the wrong debts and take the right risks and you'll have no worries. Imagine living your life in such a way that there are only three points where you have to worry about money—when you buy a house, when you buy a car, and when you go to college—and the rest of the time, you don't even think about it.

That is what we're setting out to do in this book.

No Worries is divided into five parts.

Part I is all about your attitude—are you in a place spiritually and emotionally where you are receptive to making money?

Part II is all about balance—having a healthy relationship with money.

Part III gets into the details of how you manage the stress associated with having debt, and ways to minimize it.

Part IV gets into the details of how you manage the stress associated with risk, and ways to minimize it. I introduce you to the Awesome Portfolio—a simple and powerful portfolio that builds wealth and minimizes risk stress.

Part V is about relief, and all the good things that will come your way once you succeed in minimizing your financial stress.

....

I like to tell people that I am not in the money business—I am in the happy business. *No Worries* is a book about money, yes, but it is really a book about being financially happy.

A million dollars does not guarantee happiness. Let me tell you that there are plenty of rich people with lots of financial stress, and plenty of poor people with none. That may seem hard to believe, but I know people who have made plenty more money than me, and often it makes their stress go up, not down. Your life gets infinitely more complicated. Elon Musk is the richest person in the world, or was for a time. That guy has lots of financial stress, and it is all self-inflicted.

Getting rich may get you a higher standard of living, but it may not necessarily reduce your stress. If you have bad habits, it frequently doesn't. It's a well-known fact that many lottery winners end up losing most or all their money. It's because they had crappy habits when they had no money, and more money didn't fix the crappy habits.

But when someone with good habits falls ass-backwards

into money, magical things can happen. I heard a story of a young man who won $1 million on a sports betting site on a $50 long-shot bet. He paid off his mortgage and all his debt, and put the rest in the bank, putting him in an unassailable financial position. That's how it's done.

Even if you don't get lucky, it's no big deal—the world is filled with people who grind and save $20,000 a year, put it in a tax-advantaged retirement account and have a substantial pile at the end. They don't torch their savings on the latest investment fad, like cryptocurrencies, as a contemporary example. It is much better to get rich slow—to do good work day in and day out, saving a part of what you make, investing it wisely, and watching it grow.

I came from nothing, and in middle age, I have accumulated a small fortune. Sure, I worked on Wall Street, but 90% of the money I earned was after I worked on Wall Street. Some of it was from running a successful business, and some of it was from shrewd investments.

If I can do it, you can too, and I'm not talking about the small fortune—I'm talking about achieving a lack of financial stress.

A big pile of cash is not financial freedom—I've seen plenty of people mess that up. A set of principles to deal with daily financial decisions can give you true financial freedom.

....

And there it is—*No Worries* is all about helping you to minimize your financial stress. Note that I said that the goal isn't to *eliminate* your financial stress. You can never completely eliminate it.

Part of being a human being is learning and growing and making more money and having your financial life get more and more complex. You want nice stuff, you are going to have to take a little risk, and it is going to be a little stressful.

The point is to help you eliminate *unnecessary* financial stress. Like blowing yourself up with credit card debt. Like getting buried in student loans. Like trading 3× leveraged exchange-traded funds (ETFs). Like buying too big of a house, or an extravagant car. Like being cheap. And yes, being cheap increases your financial stress, because you are *thinking* about money all the time. The goal of this book is to get you to the point where you don't even think about money—*ever*. That's next to impossible to achieve, but that is the goal.

That's why this book is for everyone—from the single mother working two jobs, to the venture capitalist decamillionaire. We're all human beings, and we have the same feelings in common. I've been on the low end, the high end, and in the middle—and I've always been able to make it work without spending a single sleepless night worrying about money.

That's what we're going to do here—we will get to a place where we hardly ever worry about money again. And I'll show you how.

....

The first chapter is the most important chapter in this book, where we will talk about your *attitudes* toward making money. Without the right attitude, all the tips and tricks in the world will be no help whatsoever.

Let's look at that now.

PART I

....

Attitude

....

CHAPTER 1

You Have to Want It

This first and most important chapter in *No Worries* is about your attitude toward making money.

As I said before, having more money doesn't necessarily reduce your financial stress—but it can make things easier.

What is the first step in getting more money? You actually have to *want* money.

Well, that seems obvious. But it's true.

Everyone wants more money, right? Yes, everyone wants more money. But some people don't want to be *seen* wanting more money. For ethical reasons.

Let me give you an example.

Why people settle for less money

Let's think about a hypothetical history professor at a university. This is a smart person, with a PhD, presumably high SAT scores. A very capable person who could work anywhere in the private sector and make more money.

But they don't. Why not?

Here are some possible reasons:

1. THEY LIKE HISTORY

This person has the ability to make more money, but chooses not to, because they really enjoy what they do. That is an economic choice. Whatever money they are giving up by not working in banking or technology, it is worth it to them in terms of some psychic benefit from being able to do what they love on a daily basis.

I get it—I worked on Wall Street for nine years, and left, because I enjoyed writing more. I still make good money as a writer, but it was worth it for me not to put up with the insane amounts of stress on Wall Street. I make less money as a writer, but I am happier.

This is a perfectly acceptable economic choice, as long as you are honest about your motivations. And people make this choice all the time.

2. THEY LIKE A FLEXIBLE WORK SCHEDULE, WORKING WITH KIDS, ETC.

Same thing. Also an economic choice that is perfectly acceptable, as long as you are honest about your motivations.

3. THEY DON'T WANT TO BE GREEDY/ CAPITALIST/ETC.

Yes, sadly, some people have ethical problems with making money, and some people have political problems with making money.

We are not going to go into great detail on this, but there are people out there who think that it is just *wrong* to make money, above and beyond what you need for the basic necessities in life. (I also found out recently that in some religious quarters, it is considered a sin to have a bigger house than you need. News to me.)

Clearly, I come down on the side of making money. But again, I don't have a problem with a different view if people are honest about their motivations.

My insides match my outsides. I am inwardly and outwardly wanting more money. And that's perfectly fine and healthy.

Let me say again: there is nothing wrong, at all, with wanting more money, houses, cars, and material possessions. It is a perfectly natural desire that we should not deny ourselves.

It comes down to:

Money is a choice.

We all get to choose how much money we have. Jeff Bezos chose how much money he has. Mother Theresa chose how much money she had. And everyone in the middle. In each case, it is a conscious choice.

Now, if you are making $70,000 a year at XYZ company or non-profit, you might be wondering how this is a choice. You get paid what you get paid.

I encourage you to think bigger.

Think bigger

1. YOU COULD GET A RAISE

This is one very simple way to get more money. Not a lot of money, but some. It is a good first step. You might be wondering how to get a raise. I will tell you how to get a raise: *bosses don't give raises to people they don't like.*

So your job—that thing you do every day—is not your job. A lot of people naively believe that if they do a good job, the best job that they possibly can, they will get paid and promoted over time, and it will all work out.

Frequently it doesn't, because your boss is a human being, and except for that one-in-a-million exceptional boss, that person is not objectively looking at your performance and giving raises to people who do the "best job," except in cases where the employee is truly exceptional and indispensable. In most cases, the boss thinks about the employees they like the best, and gives raises to them, regardless of job performance.

Your job is not your job. *Your job is to be friends with your boss.*

Go out to lunch, go golfing, do what you have to do; but if you don't have a good personal relationship with your boss, if your boss *personally dislikes you*, you are not getting a raise or a promotion.

You might say, "I'm not going to play politics!" Well, the whole world is about politics. That's the game. If you don't play the game, you're not going to get paid. Simple as that.

If it makes you feel better, you can do a good job *and* be friends with your boss.

2. YOU COULD WORK LONGER HOURS

Yes, you could work longer hours. If you're getting paid $20/hour for eight hours a day, you could work 12 hours or 16 hours. I personally like working, so if you're like me, then this is one possible solution. I mean, you could have twice as much money, which would be twice as much fun. But you would be tired. So there are trade-offs.

This does present a problem of scalability, which we will get to in a second.

3. YOU COULD GET A SECOND JOB

There have been two times in my life when I was working two different jobs. Actually, not only was I working two different jobs, but in both cases I was going to school at the same time. I was working around the clock. I loved it—it was exhilarating.

Some people call this a side hustle. You could, for example, deliver pizzas. You meet all kinds of interesting people that way. Or work the night shift in the stock room at a hospital. Or whatever. There's no downside here. You're working, you're getting out of your head, you're doing something new and interesting, and you're making money. Loads of fun.

But this also does not solve the problem of scalability, which we are coming to.

4. YOU COULD GET A DIFFERENT JOB
THAT PAYS MORE

In most US states, teachers are woefully underpaid. If you're a teacher, you've definitely made the economic choice that you're going to do something that you enjoy and make less money *on purpose*.

Let's say you get sick of it and you decide you're going to be a real estate agent. How do you become a real estate agent?

The first step might be to call up some random real estate agent (or maybe a family member or friend) and interview them about what their job entails, and what things they like about it. Ask them how to get a real estate license. Ask them how to build a business. Ask them how to market online. All that stuff. Then you go do it.

This is going to take effort.

In fact, all of these things require effort: getting a raise; working more hours; getting a new job. I can tell you one thing for certain—money is not going to simply *come to you*. You have to go out and get it. You have to take action.

Changing careers is very difficult, because our identities are tied up in what we do for a living. If you're a teacher, you help kids. You're an educator. There's a certain social currency in that, because people have respect for educators. They don't typically have respect for real estate agents.

What is that respect worth? You can quantify it. If a teacher makes $40,000/year, and a real estate agent makes $100,000/year, then the respect is worth $60,000. So again, if you decide to remain a teacher, there is nothing wrong with that—it's simply an economic choice.

Blowing up your entire identity is not the easiest thing in the world to do. Our jobs are part of our *being*, our moral fiber. It's who we are. And, you know, you get good at your job after a while, and it's a lot of work to learn a new job all over again. Changing careers is not as simple as answering a job ad—it's about changing the definition of who we are as people. It's really hard. Most people are not willing to do it.

I did it myself—I quit the United States Coast Guard and became a trader on Wall Street. Pretty big career change, right? From government service to unbridled capitalism. The only thing I had to change when I left the Coast Guard was... everything.

You are not who you think you are. You can do *anything* if you set your mind to it!

5. YOU COULD GO TO SCHOOL TO LEARN SKILLS THAT WILL GET YOU A DIFFERENT JOB THAT PAYS MORE

Going to school is a big investment. I went to business school from 1998–2001, and it cost me $45,000 (total). It was cheaper back then. I paid for $30,000 of it while I was working and attending school part-time, and I ended up with $15,000 in loans, which I paid off after my first bonus. It ended up being a pretty good investment.

That MBA was the gateway to a new career. I wouldn't have been able to work on Wall Street without it. So with a $45,000 investment, I went from making $45,000 a year to $850,000 a year in the span of about five years. That's a massive return on investment.

Nowadays, higher education is more expensive, so you have to do some *math* on whether school will help you fulfill your financial goals. Frequently it doesn't. If grad school costs $200,000 and you're going to be making $40,000 a year afterwards, that is not a good investment.

People tend to think that higher education will solve all their problems, but you have to be realistic about what you will make upon graduation. Making $40,000 after graduation is acceptable if you might make multiple six figures further down the line, but hope is not a strategy. You have to be realistic.

We will talk about how to pay for education in Chapter 10.

6. YOU COULD START INCOME INVESTING

In other words, you could be a landlord.

People *love* passive income. They want to buy up ten houses, rent them out, then sit back and collect rent checks and make $100,000 a year for doing nothing.

I have opinions on this. The passive income game is very hard. And very risky.

First of all, what a lot of people think of as passive income is actually *active* income. Pretend you're a landlord. You have to deal with clogged toilets and leaky roofs, and some drunk knucklehead that sets off all your fire extinguishers. If you have a bunch of properties, it is going to keep you busy. You are going to have to do a lot of work—it is not simply a matter of sitting back and collecting checks.

Second of all, there is a lot of risk. Typically, people buy these investment properties with leverage (meaning, they put 20% down and borrow the rest), and if you own a bunch of investment properties, you are massively exposed to the vagaries of the real estate market.

Furthermore, most people invest in real estate in a specific geographic area, so all the risk is concentrated in one place. Of course, this can also work in your favor. There are a lot of people who feel like geniuses after watching the real estate market go up in recent years. Never confuse brains with a bull market.

Remember, we had a period of time in the 2000s when real estate values went down—a lot. There is risk, and most people don't understand the risk.

But you don't have to play the passive income game with just houses; you can do it with laundromats, RV parks, self-storage units, or even dental practices. Anything that produces income will do.

I personally dislike passive income, but some people make it work. They do it in their spare time, and if they are good, they end up doing it full-time. People become millionaires by doing this. People become *billionaires* by doing this.

Like anything else, it's hard. It's never easy. But again, you can do it.

7. YOU COULD START A BUSINESS

Now we have arrived at the number one way that people make life-changing money—through entrepreneurship.

They start a business, it grows, and they sell it. It happens thousands of times each year. And I'm not talking about multibillion-dollar exits; I'm taking about plain vanilla businesses—like an HVAC company—that produce cash flows, get big, and then the founder sells for $10 million and moves to a gated community.

I'm a big proponent of entrepreneurship, for a bunch of reasons, but the biggest reason is that…

…*you will be happier.*

Working in someone else's organization can be soul-destroying. Stupid bosses, stupid politics, stupid projects, you're not in charge of your time or destiny. Yes, starting a business is risky, but I can tell you that you will be happier *even if it fails.*

Entrepreneurship is the greatest thing in the world. It's more than just not having a boss. I have had some bosses, and even the ones I disliked personally were not terrible. Building something from scratch is a life-affirming act. It's about building something with your own hands, and then getting the satisfaction—that hit of dopamine—every time you make a sale. There is nothing better than winning.

I have a successful newsletter business. I started it in the middle of the financial crisis, having walked away from millions of dollars on Wall Street. The first few months, the stock market was crashing, I had no revenue coming in, and I was so distraught that I would come to work every morning and puke in the trash can. Every single morning. Sit down in my chair, turn on the computer, and puke in the trash can. I thought I had made a terrible mistake.

Well, I made $235,000 that first year, which was very respectable under the circumstances. Now, my newsletter is a multimillion-dollar business with stable, predictable cash flows. Fifteen years later, I'm not bored with it. I still love what I do. Sure, I deal with stress from time to time, but it's a different sort of stress than I had in the past, and a lot more manageable.

Here's how people get wealthy:

1. You start a business.
2. It grows over time.
3. When you're ready, you sell it for a multiple of cash flows.

The scalable business

Now, there are hard businesses and easy businesses. Seems like everyone wants to open a restaurant. It's a very fulfilling thing to do—but not usually very profitable, unless you crush it. It's a complex business, a lot of things can go wrong, but if you do well, you get to have a decent standard of living.

I had an intern once whose ambition was to start a print magazine. Not many people are making money off of print magazines these days. That is one of those businesses that if it doesn't make money, and doesn't lose money, and you pay yourself a little along the way, then it is a success.

What I am in search of is *scalable* businesses. An internet newsletter is a scalable business. It takes the same effort to write one copy as it does a million copies. The business can grow rapidly, without much increase in overhead. If you look at all the really profitable businesses out there, they are all scalable, *weightless* businesses. "Weightless" means not much in the way of capital expenditure or assets on the balance sheet. Facebook is the ultimate example of this—it's an infinitely scalable computer program. It works the same with one user as it does with 2.6 billion users.

You can scale just about anything, but some businesses are easier to scale than others. You can scale restaurants by opening more, and having economies of scale. You can scale being a real estate agent by buying a brokerage, and hiring other agents, and taking a piece of commissions, and having economies of scale. It doesn't have to be an internet business to be scalable. There are very large roofing companies, HVAC companies, and landscaping companies that all scaled.

Of course, some people don't want to scale their businesses—they just want to have a simple contracting business and make $100,000 a year. And again, that is an economic choice. We all get to choose how much money we have. Some people are more ambitious than others.

I have some money, but I am by no means the richest person in the world. My newsletter business is not the best business in the world. Yes, it is scalable, but it grows slowly. And part of that is by choice—I don't really like marketing. So I have chosen the amount of money that I make.

We all choose the amount of money that we make.

If you wanted to figure out how to get a phone number in your bank account, I'm sure you could do it. When you see someone who is richer than you, and their life seems really easy, what you're not seeing is all the hard work and risk-taking that went into it.

It's about your mindset

Really, it's about your identity—how you view yourself. Maybe you view yourself as an average Joe/working woman/ blue-collar guy. What I am saying is that if you want to make more money, you will have to blow up your identity and think of yourself in a completely different way. And that's not easy to do. You will change the way you dress, the way you act, the way you talk, even the restaurants you go to.

But maybe you say, "I couldn't hang out with those stuck-up people." I sincerely hope that if you make a lot of money, it makes you stuck-up! Being stuck-up comes from the knowledge that you did something, and that *anyone could do what you did*—but chose not to.

That's what's at the bottom of this game—lots and lots of hard work. Most of the time, making money is hard, there are no shortcuts, it's arduous, and it's really a grind. It took my newsletter business *ten years* to really take off. If I knew how much work it would be, I might never have done it.

If you want to make money, that's what you have to look forward to. A lifetime of effort.

The alternative is that you can remain the authentic you that you are, and accept that you'll never be able to go to that nice restaurant that you've always wanted to go to.

Money is a choice: you have to choose to want it. It also

represents choices. It represents things you can do. It represents *options*.

Wealthy people have more options than the rest of us. For example, a big perk of being rich is private air travel. The ability to go to the airport, skip security, get on your own plane, and fly anywhere. I like to think of money as a big pile of things I can do. Anything becomes possible.

You must possess a belief system which tells you that material things can make you happier and that your work and effort can buy increased comfort. And if you want to make the world a better place, you can donate what's left over. When I think of making more money, that's the first thing that I think of—all the good that I can do with it. You don't have the ability to do any of these things if you don't want money.

All the personal finance lessons, stock tips, and investment research in the world won't make you rich until you first get the right attitude. And having the right attitude will dramatically reduce your financial stress. This isn't a book about getting rich, per se, but in order for this book to work, you first have to have the right mindset.

Don't get mad, get even. Go out and make more money. I just gave you an instruction manual. It's not easy, but you can do it. I have full confidence in you.

....

Next, we are moving on to Part II, which is about Balance— having a healthy relationship with money.

We begin with Chapter 2, where we talk about how wealth is a product of a few big decisions, not a million small decisions— one of the most important concepts in this book.

PART II

Balance

....

A Few Big
Decisions

Go to the personal finance section in the bookstore. What do you see?

10 Easy Steps To Become A Millionaire!

Debt is Evil! Cut Up Your Credit Cards!

Don't Buy Coffee at Starbucks!

(I'm making this up, but this is representative of the genre.)

There is a whole ecosystem of personal finance authors, bloggers, and talking heads out there. And they pretty much all say the same thing:

That whether you have money is the product of a million small decisions.

For example, my large, iced coffee from Dunkin' Donuts

costs $3.59 every day, and if I make the coffee at home, and didn't buy it at Dunkin' Donuts, I would save $3.59 a day, for 250 working days a year, which comes out to $900 a year. If I invested that $900 a year for 40 years, I would have $36,000, and with investment gains, compounded at a ridiculous 12% return assumption, I would have $200,000, and I would be well on my way to retirement, if only I gave up drinking coffee every day.

So let me say this. The math checks out. If you do this, you may end up with $200,000—assuming a lot of things go right.

But you will be miserable.

Any program that asks you to give up a very small, affordable luxury on a daily basis is not going to work. People can't sustain it over time. They will give up trying to save money, because it seems too hard, and they'll be oblivious to the real causes of their financial problems.

Piece of advice: drink the coffee if you want to.

You have these people who are, on paper, millionaires. They have two commas in the bank account. But they live in 1,200-square-foot houses, own one cheap suit, and have a 17-year-old beater car with the paint peeling off. You are living among these people—they are in your neighborhood. They are all around you. They did it—after a lifetime of austerity, after a lifetime of not drinking coffee, not buying clothes, not taking vacations, they have a million dollars or more.

And what are they doing with it?

Nothing. They are doing nothing with it. They are lousy tippers, they're the Grinch at Christmas, and they don't give to charity. They log onto the bank account every day and count their money.

Often, I find that these people all read the same books and blogs and listen to the same podcasts. And these podcasts teach that *austerity* is the solution to all your problems; if you clip coupons and buy generic-brand soup and shop for clothes at

Walmart, you will get to that magic number. And you know what, they are right!

You can earn a modest salary and get to a million dollars someday. It is totally possible.

But you will be miserable in the process.

Don't get me wrong—I'm not one of these YOLO big spender people—I'm a saver as well.

But what I want you to see is that money is not the product of a million small decisions; it's the product of just a few big decisions—and if you get the big decisions right, you won't have to worry about the small decisions.

Let me say that again, because it's worth repeating: get the big decisions right, and you won't have to worry about the small decisions.

We live in a culture that constantly tells us that it's the little things that count—make your bed every morning, and you will make good habits and have a rich and successful life. Turn off the lights when you leave a room. Fold your laundry. The Admiral McRaven commencement speech at the Naval Academy that went viral a few years ago.

But that's not true when it comes to money. The little things are little things—and don't really matter. They are inconsequential. It is the big things that matter. People get this completely backwards.

There are people who fiddle with the thermostat in order to save money. They'll turn it up to 86 degrees in the summer, and sit around, shirtless, sweating. Congratulations, you just saved $20 off your electric bill. They turn it down to 60 degrees in the winter, and wear three pairs of socks. If you keep this up over the course of a year, you will have $240, and if you do this for 40 years, you will have $10,000, plus gains on your investment. The math checks out. If you are uncomfortable for 40 years, you will have $10,000.

This is pointless asceticism that doesn't have a material impact on your financial well-being; but we have been trained to believe that if we are experiencing misery and discomfort, then we are saving money. We have been taught to believe that *unless* we are experiencing misery and discomfort, we aren't saving money. Air conditioning is the greatest thing in the world—use it. The whole point of having money is so that we don't have to feel physical discomfort.

Here's a good one—you might think that by making a pizza at home instead of ordering a pizza from Domino's, you are saving money. If you order a pizza, it's $20, but all the ingredients that go into making a pizza at home are worth $5, so you are saving money.

Except that between chopping the vegetables and grating the cheese and making the dough and baking the pizza, it's three hours of your time; so if your time is worth $25 an hour, you just spent $80 on the pizza.

There is this thing known as the division of labor—Domino's is better at making pizzas than you (and faster), so you should let Domino's make the pizza, and you can spend your time on work, or watching baseball, or virtually anything else, and it's a better use of your time, from an economic standpoint.

If you say you want to make a pizza because it's fun and it's a good thing to do with the family, or because it tastes better, then great—at least you are being honest about your intentions. But making your own pizza for the purposes of saving money is a value-destroying proposition.

This is part of a longer discussion about the relationship between time and money. Back in the mid-2000s, you had these extreme couponing shows, where someone would spend days and days clipping coupons, then go buy $500 worth of groceries for $5. They saved $495.

Except it was 100 hours' worth of work, which valued their time at $5/hour.

Time is more important than money—always. If you have the relationship between time and money backwards, you will never succeed in accumulating wealth. You can always make more money. You can't make more time.

So, what are those few big things that you need to get right?

The big things

Let's go through some numbers:

If you get a house that is $100,000 more expensive than you ordinarily would, then, at current interest rates, you will end up spending $110,000 *in interest* over the life of the mortgage. That's about *100 years* of coffee.

If you get an $80,000 car and finance it, at current interest rates, you will spend about $20,000 in interest, which is about *20 years* of coffee.

If you go to an expensive college, you could take out $300,000 in loans, which would be about five lifetimes of coffee.

There are a few things you *must* get right or you will not be financially successful:

- The house
- The car
- The student loans

Remember, this is not about being financially successful. This is about being financially *happy*. This is the way to being happy—get the big things right, and don't worry about the little things.

The reason this works is because people are more easily able to forgo large luxuries than small luxuries. You can live in a 2,500-square-foot house instead of a 3,000-square-foot. You'll still be happy. You won't be sitting in that house thinking about how miserable you are because you don't have a bigger house. You'll be perfectly happy in that house—and you will be saving $110,000 in interest. We'll have *a lot* to say about houses later.

If you buy a Toyota Yaris instead of a BMW, you won't be miserable driving your car. The average person spends 4% of their time driving a car. It's a way to get from A to B. Most car decisions are driven by ego and status (and aggressive salesmen), so if you can put your ego aside, you can get a reasonably priced car that won't financially cripple you. We will go into greater detail on buying cars later in the book.

And finally, do not go to schools that you can't afford. If the tuition bill for a private university will be multiple six figures, think about going to a state school and getting in-state tuition. Or go to community college for two years and transfer to a four-year school later. I have a rubric for how to afford college that you will read about later in the book.

If you do these three things—*if you get these three big things right*—you will lead a stress-free financial life. And you won't have to worry about the coffee, or the thermostat, or anything else.

If you don't do these three things—if you make a mistake with the house, the car, or the student loans—then it can cost you a comfortable retirement, or worse.

People aren't appropriately nervous when they are buying a house or a car. You should be. If you get this wrong, you could be financially hobbled—for life. When you're signing the loan documents for a mortgage, your hands should be shaking. If they're not, then you don't grasp the magnitude of the situation.

The exception

Now, there are people out there who truly do have spending problems. They spend too much. And correspondingly, there are people out there who spend too little.

People can become addicted to all sorts of things—alcohol, drugs, gambling, sex—and buying something produces the same dopamine hit that these other things do. People can also become addicted to spending money.

Typically, in these situations, the personal finance expert prescribes some program of discipline. Some mechanical method by which people can put money in envelopes or whatever, make budgets, and stick to the plan. But this doesn't work on people who have real spending addictions. Discipline isn't going to make an alcoholic not drink. These people need intensive therapy to solve their problems, or something else. So that is outside the scope of this discussion.

Besides, I am not a big fan of rules. People like rules—because it absolves them from any responsibility to think. I prefer *principles*. If you have a heuristic that says, "Save as much as possible," that is preferable to a complex series of rules.

I don't spend a lot of money outside of the occasional vacation or clothes purchase, and it's not because I'm obeying a system of rules. I know that the less money I spend, the more money I can save, which I can use to buy something I *really* want in the future. Otherwise known as: delayed gratification. Note: the future will come someday, and you can spend that money.

Someone who is an average spender, or even an above-average spender, will still be able to save and invest, as long as they get the three big things right.

You may already be thinking about what the three big things have in common. Yes, it's *debt*.

Debt is one of the two sources of financial stress, which we discuss in the next chapter.

CHAPTER 3

....

The Two Sources of Financial Stress

T he purpose of this book is to help you to minimize financial stress.

There are *only* two sources of financial stress: debt and risk. There are no other sources of financial stress. All financial stress can be boiled down to debt or risk.

It's worth repeating: not having money is not a source of financial stress. There are a lot of broke, perfectly happy people out there. I am envious of them, actually. Their lives are so uncomplicated. And as we will discuss in the next chapter, not having enough money is a solvable problem.

The first source of financial stress is debt.

Debt is a source of financial stress

I'm not one of these people who say that debt is evil—you can accomplish a lot of good things with debt—but I do say that it can significantly ramp up your financial stress.

When you have debt, you have a fixed payment that you need to meet every month. This causes stress. If you don't have debt, you don't have payments, and you have no stress. Simple as that. Debt is a source of stress.

In my life, I have owned five houses—and had a mortgage on four of them. One of the houses I bought with cash—it was a cheap house. And it was then that I learned that having no debt is the greatest thing in the world. I actually wasn't debt-free at the time—I had a car loan that I was paying—but not having a mortgage on the house was simply amazing. The house was *mine*. There was no way I could lose it, outside of some horrific accident that saddled me with millions in medical bills. I didn't have a few thousand being sucked out of my bank account every month. All I had to pay was the insurance and property taxes.

In 2015, I bought another house, and got a mortgage this time. I paid it off three and a half years later. Yes—I paid off my mortgage in 3.5 years. I so enjoyed the feeling of not having any debt on my previous house that I was in a big hurry to pay it off. So I did. Today, I don't have any debt—none whatsoever. No payments. No worrying about making payments.

Not having any debt has made me *happy*.

I hear stories about people who lay awake at night wondering how they are going to pay all the bills. They are low on cash, and they start prioritizing what bills they are going to pay. Gotta pay the mortgage—can't lose the house. Gotta pay the car loan—need to drive around. Usually, it is the credit cards that people fall behind on, and then things get ugly. The interest compounds, and the credit card debt spirals out of control. This scene is played out millions of times a year in the United States.

If you have less debt, you have smaller payments—simple as that. A smaller mortgage will mean smaller payments. You shouldn't have a car loan in the first place—financing a rapidly depreciating asset is a terrible idea, as we will see in Chapter 11—but if you do, it should be small, at a low interest rate. Of course, lots of people's student loan payments are small, because of income-based repayment plans, which is actually counterproductive; but we will talk about that later in the book as well.

Is the goal to eliminate all debt?

Ultimately, yes. Some debt is better than others—mortgage debt is better than car loans, which is better than credit cards, which is better than student loans. You can pay the mortgage off last. But when you eliminate these payments one by one, you will experience existential joy that transcends the dopamine hit you get when you buy something. The payment will disappear, and the free cash you are earning will flow directly to equity—your net worth.

WHAT IS DEBT?

What is debt, philosophically speaking?

You borrow money, and interest is the penalty you pay for consuming something today instead of waiting until tomorrow. Conversely, when you save money, interest is the reward you earn for postponing consumption until tomorrow.

If you have a mortgage on your house, you don't really own

the house—the bank does. If you have a loan on your car, you don't really own the car—the bank does.

In the case of cars, this is absolutely true—if you have a car loan, the bank is actually in possession of the title to the car, and you don't get the title until you pay off the car loan. I found this out in 2015—I got a car loan from USAA for a Toyota Highlander, and when the loan was paid in full, I got an envelope in the mail with my title in it. It took me a minute to figure out what was going on.

Imagine going through life and never really owning anything. You have debt on your house and your car. Maybe you are one of these people who finances their refrigerator and washer/dryer. If you don't own anything, you don't own your life—you are always working for someone else. You are an employee of the bank, and the interest that you pay goes to bank profits. I like banks, and a sound banking system is good for a healthy economy, but I'm not in the mood to make bank profits bigger than absolutely necessary.

The reality is that it is hard to go through life without ever using debt. Not many houses are bought with cash (especially for first-time homebuyers). Nine out of ten cars are financed. People should really get into the habit of buying cars with cash, but the price of new and used cars has increased so much that it's virtually impossible. I get it. While the goal should be to eliminate debt over time, invariably you are going to have to use some here and there along the way. And the goal should be to get out of it as quickly as possible.

THE CERTAIN RETURN FROM
PAYING OFF DEBT

I come from a Wall Street background, and the Wall Street folks that I work with absolutely do not understand my philosophy on debt. They are confounded by it. For example, if you can get a mortgage at 4% and you have a choice of paying down the mortgage or investing in the stock market for a potential return of 8%, why on earth would you pay down the mortgage? It makes no economic sense.

I agree—on the surface, it would seem to make very little economic sense.

But if you pay down your mortgage, you are earning a *certain* return of 4%. And returns in the stock market are *uncertain*. Sometimes it is 8%, sometimes less, sometimes more. It is true that the stock market has historically returned 8%, but we don't know—we really don't know—what it will do in the future. It's a decision theory problem—would you rather take a certain 4% paying down the mortgage, or an uncertain 8% in the stock market?

Keep in mind that even though the stock market returns 8% a year, most people end up making much less than that, because of suboptimal behavior. They become overly optimistic when stocks go up, and overly pessimistic when stocks go down. Something we will cover in detail later in the book.

Most of all, the reason to pay down the mortgage instead of investing in the stock market is to *reduce stress*. And you're still investing in an asset—it's just real estate, instead of stocks. And who knows—maybe the real estate will have a higher rate of return.

Of course, there is a balance. You can't divert *all* your cash to debt reduction—you need to invest early and often in your various retirement accounts so the returns compound over time. Most people would rather invest than pay down debt—because investing is fun! Buy a stock, watch it go up, you feel like a genius. Everyone loves to punt around stocks and mutual funds. Most of the trading activity out there is purely recreational. The research shows that people would be better off in index funds, but that hasn't dissuaded millions of people from getting Robinhood accounts and punting around GameStop and AMC. Huge amounts of fun.

Not so much fun to pay down your mortgage—what do you get for that? Just the satisfaction that you're chipping away at this mountain of debt over time, with the knowledge that by reducing your debt, you will reduce your stress, and achieve peace and serenity. That sounds a lot better to me.

Paying down your mortgage is boring, I get it. It's like picking out tube socks. But I assure you, the satisfaction you get at the end is not boring.

The second source of financial stress is risk.

Risk is a source of financial stress

There are all different kinds of risk in the world. We will confine our discussion to financial risk—and specifically financial market risk.

Pretty much everyone knows what a stock is—it is shares in a company. If you buy a stock, you are a part owner in a company. So far, so good.

Stocks tend to go up over time. Sometimes they go down, and sometimes they go down a lot, but usually they go up. This is a true statement.

The United States is a very peculiar place. It is the only place in the world where people trust their retirement savings—their *life* savings—to the stock market. Nobody else does this. Europe doesn't do this—European stocks have essentially returned zero for the last 15 years. Japan doesn't do this. Japanese stocks have had negative returns for the last 30 years. The U.S. is the only place where people *trust* the stock market as a long-term investment vehicle. They trust it so much that in 2005, President George W. Bush, along with Treasury Secretary John Snow, proposed a scheme to invest Social Security contributions in the stock market. People freaked out. That's where we draw the line, apparently.

The United States is a country of crazy gamblers. Why? Because we invest all our money in stocks, and every ten years or so a giant tsunami of a bear market crashes the stock market down 50%. And then the stock market comes back. This is the way we've done things for the last 100 years. It's nuts.

I don't like volatility. It makes me nervous. It stresses me out. Stocks go up, stocks go down, and you log into the app for your brokerage account and it's moving around thousands of dollars at a time. Does that make you nervous? It makes me nervous. Most of the time, I don't even log in.

The purpose of volatility is to make people make stupid decisions.

Stocks go up, and you are happy. Stocks go down, and you are unhappy. Stocks go down even more, and you are suicidal. Eventually you can't take it anymore, and you sell all your stocks on the lows… and then they go up again. Then you buy them back higher… and they go down. This is why the typical individual investor massively underperforms the market.

This wouldn't happen in 1984. In 1984, you could get an interest rate of 8% in a savings account. You get 8% a year, guaranteed—no volatility, and none of the emotions that are associated with it. You leave the money in the bank, and it compounds over time.

Here is most of the personal finance advice I see these days:

> Invest all your money in aggressive growth stock mutual
> funds, because they return the most.

This is the most simplistic, stupidest thing I have ever heard, divorced from reality, and completely ignorant of decades of financial history.

Here's what the textbooks tell us:

> If something returns a lot, it probably also has a lot of
> risk. Loosely translated, it has a lot of volatility.

Yes, aggressive growth stocks have historically returned the most, but at a cost: obscene amounts of volatility. *And the purpose of volatility is to make people make stupid decisions.*

You stick people in ridiculously volatile stocks, the first time the stock market drops 30%, they're going to panic, and liquidate everything. I've been investing for 24 years. I see it over and over again. You can tell people to "hang on" as much as you want, you can try to behaviorally condition them into making the right decisions, but they mess it up every time.

The lesson here is that it is not just the expected returns that count, but the path you take to get there. This is known as *path dependency*.

An asset that goes up 4% in straight-line fashion is potentially more valuable than an asset that goes up 8% with lots of volatility. Why? Because we're human beings and we have *emotions*, and we are all hard-wired to be terrible investors.

People are advised to *dollar-cost average*, which is to send in a fixed amount of money to the mutual funds in good times and in bad times—but in bad times, most people get scared and stop contributing; and in good times, they get excited and contribute more, so they are synthetically buying the highs and selling the lows. *This* is why investors don't realize those average 8% returns of the market.

The goal of any investment strategy should be to target risk first, and returns second. Because risk is the second source of financial stress. You can't fully eliminate risk—that would not be desirable, because your returns would be zero and you would have to work like hell to save for retirement. But you can't fully embrace risk, either.

On occasion, things in the financial markets get really, really bad. Remember what it was like in the Great Financial Crisis? When bank stocks were trading in the low single digits? When we thought we were going into a full-fledged Depression? That will happen again, I assure you. You may think that you can ride it out, and keep sending in those checks to your mutual fund. You will not. You will crap your pants, because that is what human beings are hard-wired to do.

The sources of all financial stress are debt and risk

As I mentioned previously, the source of financial stress is *not* not having enough money. There are lots of people with no money who have no financial stress—they have no debt and they have no risk.

The goal isn't to be rich—the goal is to be happy; though if you're doing it right, you can probably have it both ways. I know rich people who are profoundly unhappy. I know poor people who are deliriously happy. The happy ones, rich and poor, have minimized their debt and risk—without fail.

This is one of the reasons I can't get my head around bitcoin. Yes, the returns were phenomenal for a time, but it's the riskiest asset in existence. I owned it for a while, and did well, but I found that I spent all day staring at the price. When I finally sold it, I let out a huge sigh of relief. I didn't have to worry about it anymore. Bitcoin was causing me *stress*. I could not have been happier to be done with it.

Some people are wired differently—some people are risk-seeking as opposed to risk-averse. They buy the riskiest stocks and crypto and build the most volatile portfolio imaginable. They're gamblers. And the stock market does serve that function for some people—they get a "fix" from the volatility. They always need to have some action.

If you're one of those people, my suggestion is to take $500 and go to the craps table, and have some fun. In your real financial life, with your life savings, build a portfolio that doesn't make you puke in the trash can every ten years. I'll show you how to do that in Part IV.

Look, I could write a book about how to get the most money in the bank. Throughout my career, I have been exposed to some very wealthy people—including billionaires—and I know about their beliefs and their habits. I know the things they did to get rich. You can imitate those habits, and get rich. There are already a lot of those books out there, though.

But the goal is not to be a billionaire. The goal is to be happy. You should never worry about money—there are better things in this world to be worrying about than money. You should worry about your marriage, your kids, your job, your father with Alzheimer's who refuses to sign a power of attorney, your beloved cat who was just diagnosed with lymphoma. Those are the right things to worry about—not money. Worrying about money is stupid. Financial stress compounds all other stresses and makes them intolerable. And financial stress is typically man-made—it is a problem of our own creation. It is completely avoidable.

Not only should you not worry about money, on any given day, you should not even *think* about money, except to reach into your wallet to get cash to pay for lunch—and then not think about it again for the rest of the day. If you're not thinking about money, then your mind is freed up to think about all kinds of other things, and you can be much more productive and happy.

Next, we will learn about how it makes more sense to focus on revenues than expenses, which is another great way to reduce your financial stress.

CHAPTER 4

....

The Revenue Side

The Greatest Lie Ever Told:

You can get rich by cutting expenses to the bone.

Austerity is tough. It's tough to maintain day after day, week after week, month after month. And it's even tougher to maintain over 40 years.

This program that you are signing up for—denying yourself simple, common luxuries that everyone else has, for an entire lifetime—is too hard. Yes, some people do it, and they do it successfully. But it results in unnecessary suffering and deprivation, and more importantly, distorts your relationship with money.

When you live this way, money is not your friend, it is your master. And every decision, no matter how small—such as whether to get a soda out of a vending machine—must be examined within the following framework: *Do I need it?*

We are constantly told that we buy stuff we don't need. So? Sometimes we buy things because it is fun. And sometimes we buy a drink because we are thirsty, because waiting two hours to get a drink at home will result in unnecessary discomfort. Money may not make us happy, but it does make things easier. Even people who are indigent can buy a soda out of the vending machine. But this is the mental math that these cheapskates do on a daily basis, 10–20 times a day.

Any program that asks you to deny yourself small, affordable luxuries for a period of months, years, or decades is doomed to fail. Because there are two possible outcomes: either you won't be able to do it, and you will give up on your financial future; or you will be able to do it, and you will be miserable and make everyone else around you miserable, too. Nothing good will come of this.

When I was in my 20s, I discovered an important concept known as the *revenue side*. It's one of those things that, once you see it, you can't unsee it.

How I discovered the revenue side

Let me tell you a story.

I served in the United States Coast Guard from 1992–2001. First, I was a cadet at the Coast Guard Academy, and then I was a commissioned officer. By the time I separated from the Coast Guard, aged 27, I was making about $45,000 a year.

Now, at the time, I was already very frugal, but I suppose it would have been possible to squeeze out an additional $2,000 to $3,000 a year in expenses. But instead of thinking about cutting expenses, I thought instead about increasing *revenue*. I decided to change careers, to something that paid a bit more. So I finished my MBA, applied for employment at several large Wall Street firms, and got a job at one of the biggest. Within five years, I was making $850,000 a year.

The most elegant solution to the problem of not having enough money is... to make more money.

There is a mythology in the U.S. about the YOLO free spender who, with a 580 credit score, gets a $80,000 Chevy Silverado with 100% financing. Those people do exist, but in my experience, they are rarer than we are led to believe. Most people are actually pretty good with money. And most people are actually pretty frugal. Most people make budgets, buy stuff on sale, and cut unnecessary expenses.

But what they don't do is try to make more money.

Cutting expenses is not fun, but making more money is huge amounts of fun. I shared some ideas on how to do this in Chapter 1. If you make money by working, then generally you make more money by working more. This is not hard to figure out.

Your household is not too different from a corporation. Corporations have revenues and expenses. Revenues are easy to understand—that's what they get from selling their products or services. Expenses are things like payroll, administration, marketing, things like that. Revenues minus expenses equals profit—nothing complicated about that.

You also have revenues—what you make in W-2 or business income—and expenses—food, vacations, kids' clothes, etc. If you have money left over after your expenses, that's money in the bank.

Now, corporations do occasionally cut expenses—for example, they can lay off employees. They typically only do this when business is contracting. But during periods of expansion, they're focusing on the *revenue side*—how much they can sell. The analysts at Wall Street firms who analyze stocks pay more attention to revenue than anything else—*is the business growing?* You don't find too many large corporations that try to increase their market value by solely focusing on expenses.

And you shouldn't, either. If you think about your household as a business, the first question you should ask yourself is: is the business growing? Are you making more money year after year? Is your *revenue* growing? How fast is it growing?

I can tell you this: Jeff Bezos has never once thought about whether to get a soda out of the vending machine. It is a dollar. He can always make another dollar. You're the same—you can always make more money.

Focusing on the revenue side involves *risk*—something some people are uncomfortable with. It is a small risk to ask for a raise, I suppose. You might annoy your boss. But really, the worst that can happen is that he says no. It is a bigger risk to look for another job, or to change careers. Yes, you might fail. The alternative is that you can sit in your stultifying cube farm every day and read about people getting rich on the internet.

People get stuck. Stuck is a very bad place to be. The way to get unstuck is to take action. You've probably had at least one good business idea in your life. Why didn't you do it? Too hard. There is a lot involved. Say you wanted to start a tattoo removal business. You have to form an LLC, get the necessary permits, find a piece of real estate, pay rent, hire employees, lease the equipment, get an accounting system, open a bank account—all that stuff.

Maybe you looked at Facebook and said, "Dang, that is a pretty good idea for a business—why didn't I think of that?"

The idea is worth next to nothing. It is all in the execution. You have to go out there and *do stuff*. You solve one problem, and you solve another problem, and after you've solved all the problems that you can possibly solve, you get to sit on top of a big pile of cash.

I worked on Wall Street in its wildest, most exciting time. Nobody was worried about expenses at the big banks—we used to get yelled at if we didn't spend *enough* money. Not coincidentally, those were very successful businesses. Then, the financial crisis happened, and the culture changed—the banks became focused on expenses, and they have never recovered. As a vendor, I can attest that they will now haggle over $100. And the business has suffered. They are no longer dynamic, risk-taking entities. In the 2000s, they would spend money on technology, payroll, and client entertainment—because they always knew they would make more. Now, no more holiday parties. Make sure you work in an industry that still has holiday parties.

Focus on the revenue side, not the expense side.

An abundance mentality

What this really comes down to is the difference between a *scarcity mentality* and an *abundance mentality*.

A scarcity mentality says that there is not enough pie to go around, so we have to ration it very carefully. The idea that there is only a finite amount of money in the world is absurd. First of all, we print more of it all the time, without getting into the ethics or politics of that. Second of all, wealth is not a static quality that is moved from one pile to the next, or looted or plundered. It is something that can be created. When a successful company reaches a $90 billion private valuation, that hasn't come at the expense of something else—it was literally created out of thin air. It was created by the founders and employees of that business who created something of great value that has grown over time.

Instead of trying to slice and dice the pie into smaller and smaller pieces, why not just make the pie bigger? This is an abundance mentality.

At the end of this is a reward: once you get there, you will no longer have to worry about money. All the time that you spend thinking about it right now, all the financial decisions you have to make over the course of a week, you will never have to worry about making those decisions again. You will achieve a state of plenty.

You can go out to dinner and not have to run through all these calculations as to how much you are going to have left over at the end of the month. You just pay the bill, get in your car, and leave.

But you can't get there by carefully cutting uncanceled stamps off envelopes, which is what my family used to do circa 1984.

Like I said, I could have tried to scrounge up an extra $2,000 when I was 27 years old, and if I had saved $2,000 a year for 40 years, I would have had $80,000, assuming I just plunked it in a bank account. But instead, I decided to make *more money*. And it was not easy.

There was a period of time when I was working my Coast Guard job, my trading floor job, and going to grad school—all at the same time. I was sleeping—I kid you not—two hours a night. After a year of this, I was delirious from lack of sleep. Plus, I was flying back and forth to New York a few times a year to do informational interviews and make connections—all while maintaining a straight-A average. It was the hardest I have ever worked in my life—and, not coincidentally, the happiest time in my life. And the reward at the end of it was massive.

To this day, I still try to make more money at every opportunity. I am an author, the editor of a few financial newsletters, a former opinion columnist, a podcaster, and a former radio show host. Every day, I am spraying gigabytes of content across the internet. I hope to make lots of money off this book—just being honest, here.

It has been a long time since I worried about expenses.

I remember the point in my life when I stopped worrying about expenses. It was 2012, and I had taken a business trip to San Francisco. I was there for a while. I had some time to kill, so I walked down to Union Square to check out the luxury stores. I walked into the Prada store. Now, I had never been in a Prada store in my entire life. I didn't know what Prada was. But I was in this store and I looked on the shelf and saw the coolest pair of boots I had ever seen. I inspected the price tag: $1,000.

Now at that point in my life, I was 38 years old, and making about $400,000 a year. Not rich by any stretch of the imagination. And I certainly didn't *need* $1,000 boots. I don't remember what shoes I was wearing at the time; they were probably middlebrow $100 Johnston & Murphy shoes or something like that. But at that moment, I had confidence. I had confidence that my business would continue to grow, that I would continue to earn more and more money, and that I would ultimately be wildly successful.

I bought the boots. And that was the day that I switched from a scarcity mentality to an abundance mentality.

I wore those things all over the place. I still have them today. I don't wear them much anymore, but I hold onto them as a reminder of the day that I stopped being cheap and started acting like a normal human being. Not that everyone should buy $1,000 footwear, but at my income level at the time, I could afford it. The boots made me happy.

Apart from the boots, I still don't spend a great deal of money. I calculated recently that my discretionary expenses add up to about $100,000 a year—just a small fraction of what I make. In some respects, I still live below my means. It wasn't until age 47 that I decided to buy an expensive car—after I was a millionaire many times over.

You shouldn't use the abundance mentality as an excuse for free-spending ways. "I'm going to spend money, because I can always make more money!" That is true. But there are some basic personal finance habits that you should get into (that we will discuss later in this book), so that you're not an idiot with your money. You shouldn't be getting car loans with double-digit interest rates. You shouldn't be maintaining large balances on your credit cards. Etc.

....

I was in Nashville in early 2021 and went to a comedy club and saw the comedian Godfrey. He was making fun of rich people. "You ever notice that with rich people, everything is so easy?" And then he did this impersonation of a slack-jawed rich person inviting you to his tennis club or something like that.

He's onto something.

For rich people, things really are easy. They don't have this constant oppressive worry about how they're going to pay their bills, how they're going to make ends meet. When you take that out of your psyche, there is room for a lot of other things. You have room to be generous, for starters. You're relaxed and happy. The primary benefits of being rich are psychological, not the Richard Mille watch that you're going to buy. It's peace of mind, but it's more than that. A rich person believes that even if he lost everything, it's not the end of the world; he'd be able to make it all back. There is literally nothing to worry about.

All of this only works if you are focusing on the revenue side and adopt an abundance mentality. You don't get there by trying to squeeze the salt out of a biscuit. Which brings me to the concept of *upside*—something I cannot live without.

Upside

Upside is the idea that there is potentially no limit to how much money you can make. If you are a government employee, you do not have much upside. You traded it away for safety and security. If you are a teacher, you do not have much upside. If you are a real estate agent, you have considerable upside, depending on how much you want to grow your business, and how hard you want to work. If you are an investment portfolio manager, you have lots of upside. If you are a tech entrepreneur, you have virtually limitless upside. I couldn't bear the thought that there might be a limit to how much money I could make in a year, or over the course of my lifetime.

The one thing that I have in common with all my friends on Wall Street is that we all have enormous upside. We're traders, or entrepreneurs, or in businesses that have the potential to grow considerably. None of us would be content with a 9-to-5 job. I once had a friend who was the most ambitious person I knew. He worked in commercial real estate. He told me repeatedly that one day he would be a billionaire. It was a credible threat. And let me tell you, this guy was not paying too much attention to the expense side. He spent money freely, because he always knew that there would be more.

Most people have a job and make a salary and they are

constrained by what they make in their salary. If they make $80,000 a year, they have to mind expenses. My guess is that it never occurred to them to make more money. Asking for a raise is a necessary first step. It is necessary, but not sufficient. You want to get yourself into a position where you have upside. Oftentimes that means getting *equity* in the company where you work, so you can share in the profits. If the company grows, then you benefit along with it. If you're not an owner, you're simply an employee, and you're limited by whatever your boss feels like paying you.

The longer I am alive, the more I realize that a job with the government, an educational institution, or a private business that does not offer equity to employees is a really unattractive proposition. It puts you in the scarcity mentality, where you are fighting for inconsequential amounts of money.

Another way to get exposure to upside is by owning stocks. Stocks can theoretically go to infinity. Most of them don't, but if you have a portfolio of 30 of them, one or two of them might go up a lot. I've heard some stories in the last few years of people who put everything they had in a single stock—and became millionaires many times over. That's bad risk management, which we will discuss later in the book—but it serves to illustrate the point that everyone should have some exposure to upside.

Interestingly, another way to get exposure to upside is... to play the lottery. I have rather unconventional ideas about the lottery. It should be viewed as an *entertainment expense*. If you buy a Powerball ticket, what happens next? You spend the rest of the week dreaming about what you will do with the money when you win. You'll buy a luxury condo in Miami, you'll fly private, etc. This is good, clean fun. I buy Powerball tickets from time to time—ten at a clip, for $20—and then my wife and I spend the next three days imagining what we will do with the money. Like any expense, it has to fit in the budget—the rule is that you can spend 0.1% of your income on gambling or lottery tickets. So if you have a household income of $100,000, you can spend $100 on lottery tickets. Lotteries are a regressive, stupid tax, but they're fun. It's no different than buying movie tickets.

You are probably not going to win... but you might! One thing is for certain—you won't win if you don't buy a ticket. Hence, the exposure to upside. You want to be *positively exposed to luck.*

I have a rational, empirical mind, but I think luck is real. Luck is the propensity for good things to happen more often to you than other people. Luck exists—I have seen it in my career. I am the luckiest person in the world—I firmly believe that. But I also put myself in a position where I can be positively exposed to luck.

Luck

One thing I hear pretty frequently is that so-and-so billionaire is only a billionaire because they are lucky. Absolutely not true. It is very hard to make a billion dollars, and do you know what is even harder than making a billion dollars? Hanging onto a billion dollars. It's one thing to make it, but then you have to keep it! Billionaires are many things, but they are not lucky—at least, not in the sense that a billion dollars fell in their lap.

I am not a billionaire. But I am very, very lucky, mostly because I have put myself in situations where I was positively exposed to luck.

I essentially got a job at Lehman Brothers because I had hustled a job as a clerk on the floor of the Pacific Coast Options Exchange. How did I get that job? Well, I went to the career center at my school and looked up a guy that was a market maker on the exchange, and set up a meeting. I went down to the floor—a dark, musty place with lots of computer screens and people yelling unintelligible things—and talked to him for about 15 minutes. Afterwards, I asked him if I could hang out on the floor and check things out.

I brought a notepad with me, and I was writing down the names of every firm I saw—I figured I would call them later. Just then, out of the corner of my eye, a water bottle whizzed toward my head. One of the traders was trying to throw it in the trash can and almost hit me instead.

A short guy standing next to me started jumping up and down. "That guy's going to kill you! He's a freaking Marine!" He was referring to my high-and-tight haircut.

Then he turns to me. "Are you looking for a job?" he asks? "Yes, I am," I replied. "Good, I'm going to take you to a guy. Shake his hand and take his business card, then call him tomorrow." So that's what happened. He walked me across the floor to a red-haired, middle-aged man, I shook his hand, took his business card, and called him the next day.

A few days later I ended up in an interview in his office. It consisted of only a few questions. Shortly afterwards, I learned that I was hired.

I got a job on the trading floor because I was almost hit with a water bottle.

Or:

I got a job on the trading floor because I went down to the trading floor and put myself in a position where something good could happen.

That chance encounter changed the course of my entire life. It is the reason I am writing this book today. If it never happened, who knows what I'd be doing. Toiling in anonymity, probably.

I can tell you for certain that would *never* have happened if I was sitting in my apartment. Luck never finds you there.

Three ideas that will change your life

All of this ties together—focusing on the revenue side, getting exposure to upside, and being positively exposed to luck. These three ideas will change your life.

People view their financial lives very narrowly: "I go to work and do a job, I get a paycheck, and I go home." It is true what they say: the rich definitely get richer. But why do the rich get richer? Because they:

- focus on the revenue side;
- get exposure to upside; and
- are positively exposed to luck.

In the course of my career, I have seen a lot of smart, talented people with great business ideas. I've had the opportunity to invest in many of them. I've had that opportunity by virtue of the connections I've made over the years, and I've made those connections because I'm constantly striving to make my world bigger.

One chance meeting can change your whole life. One moment in time. But you have to be emotionally available for it.

Upon reading this, I hope you realize the sheer pointlessness of giving up your Dunkin' Donuts coffee in the morning.

Please focus your attention on the next chapter, where we talk about the two worst types of people in personal finance: CFs and High Rollers.

CHAPTER 5

....

CFs and
High Rollers

Back in the early 2000s, I went to a barbershop in New Jersey. It was an interesting barbershop, to say the least. All the barbers were drag queens, and used to perform shows in the West Village in New York City. One of them went as Cher, and to say that he was passable as Cher would be an understatement. If I saw him walking down the street, I would have thought it was Cher. My own barber went as Liza Minelli.

These guys had a fun working environment, goofing around and playing pranks on people. Once they put a remote-control fart machine in a potted plant outside and would let one rip anytime someone walked by. They put rubber dog poop out on the sidewalk. I loved going there—it was huge amounts of fun.

NO WORRIES | Jared Dillian

Haircuts at the time were $14. I made a habit of tipping $4, for a total of $18. I thought that was a generous tip at the time—about 30%—but today, I tip much more than that for haircuts. Out of all the service people you encounter in your life, hairstylists are the most important. More on tipping shortly.

After the haircut, I was invited in the side room to pay. Invariably, the appointment book would be left out, with people's names written in it. Next to some of the names were the letters "CF."

"What does CF stand for?" I asked.

"Cheap f**k," the barber said.

Well, I was thankful that there wasn't a "CF" next to my name—that would have been mortifying. We had a good laugh about it.

But what level of tipping earned someone the "CF" designation? Was it $2? $3? Was it zero? And it got me thinking—the difference between a CF and a reasonable tipper was perhaps just a dollar. A dollar could be all it took to earn you a reputation as someone who tipped generously.

In this chapter, we'll look at the two ends of the spectrum: CFs and high rollers. We'll see how neither is the right way to achieve a stress-free financial life and, not surprisingly, the middle ground is where to be.

The personal finance orthodoxy

A great deal of the personal finance literature in existence today turns people into CFs. It teaches people to view money as a zero-sum game—if you have more of it, I have less of it.

I'm sure you know people who are tight with a buck. Hard to deal with, right? At the time of writing, I am setting up an informal poker game at my house, $100 buy-in, cash game. One guy is a legendary CF and will not come. But that's just the tip of the iceberg. You go out to drinks every week with a bunch of people from work, and there's that one guy who never pays. Alligator arms. Believe me, I know—that used to be me. The idea of handing over $70 for other people's drinks caused me deep psychic pain.

And then you realize: it just does not matter.

Where does this come from? It comes from books like *The Millionaire Next Door*, which is a series of vignettes about people who lived in 1,200-square-foot houses, drove 20-year-old cars, and had one $99 suit—and had a seven-figure bank account.

This has led us to believe that the best and only way to become a millionaire is through years of being cheap.

But as we know, it's not what we do on the expense side that matters; it's what we do on the revenue side that matters.

The personal finance orthodoxy always sets up the *high roller* as the villain—the person with a credit score in the 500s, with tens of thousands of dollars of credit card debt, and a pile of unpaid cable bills in their kitchen drawer. This person is said to be the source of all our problems, with our consumer culture and our credit card debt. These people are living beyond their means and mortgaging their future. That's America—a bunch of sybaritic debt monkeys.

And yes, there are people like that. Lots of them. There are lots and lots of *high rollers*, the people who spend too much. And their lives are filled with financial turmoil.

But you can actually have the opposite problem, and the opposite problem is the person who spends *too little*. That person isn't at risk of going bankrupt, but they are going to have different sorts of problems. They will have relationship problems—CFs are infuriating to deal with. They will be lousy tippers. They will send their kids to a less good school instead of paying for a private school, even when they have the means to do so. This results in strained relationships, and unhappy kids.

The goal is to be somewhere in between—and have a healthy relationship with money. But when people seek guidance on personal finance, typically they are presented with extreme solutions, because extreme solutions are easy to understand and sell.

Think about how ludicrous it is that people are being taught to cut up their credit cards and live off the grid, using only cash. That is not a habit of highly effective people. And we demonize the high roller, saying that he is responsible for the terrible state of household finances in this country. I know some high rollers, including some people who have lived on the edge, coming close to missing payments, but the only visible consequence of their behavior is that their retirements will be less luxurious than most. It's not a great system—they end up paying a lot of interest, and saving and investing less than they should, and it's not a system that I would choose, but it works for them, even though they end up with less money in the end.

Materialism is good

The main thing that the CFs get wrong is that they fail to recognize a simple principle: material things bring us happiness. Sure, material things are not the only things that bring us happiness, but they do bring us happiness. It is a natural human desire to accumulate material possessions. People get in trouble when they try to subvert that desire. People tell themselves that they are actually happier without material possessions, that their spiritual needs are more important than their material needs. Maybe so. But people still have material needs.

Enter the FIRE program.

FIRE stands for Financial Independence, Retire Early. The idea is that you lead a life of asceticism for a period of 10–15 years when you graduate from college, save up over a million dollars, then retire at age 35—to pursue your dream, whatever that is— and spend the rest of your life in deprivation trying to make the million dollars last until you die. It is the dumbest thing I have ever seen. But lots of young people are doing this—they live in a tiny house or a van, spend no money, ride around on an electric bike, and say that this is the solution to all our financial problems, if only people consumed nothing and saved everything.

I disagree. I don't want to live in deprivation for 15 years so that I can live in deprivation for the next 40 years. The FIRE people claim to be free from the need to accumulate material possessions—but you can't fight human nature. There is nothing inherently wrong with consumption, but we are constantly taught that consumption is *evil*, that it's wrong to buy stuff, it's wrong to experience pleasure by buying things—it's all just going to end up in the landfill eventually, so what is the point?

Yes, there are other pleasures in life that are more fulfilling than buying the latest phone. The pleasure of a romantic relationship, for starters. The bond that parents have with their children. The relationships that we form with pets, religion and spirituality, community service—all of these things bring our life more meaning than buying a fancy shirt with a usable life of about seven years.

But we're not monks. The Gandhi thing is not for everyone. Some people say they like to keep their lives simple, and have as few possessions as possible. I say there is nothing wrong with complexity—as you get older and make more money, you buy more and more stuff to put in bigger and bigger houses. That's life. There are no good guys and bad guys here, just competing philosophies.

The middle way

The right way is the *middle* way, which requires you to have a healthy relationship with money. You save some, you spend some, and you don't spend much time thinking about it.

The thing that both CFs and high rollers both have in common is that they are ruled by money.

How do you know when you are ruled by money? When you spend all your time thinking about it. CFs and high rollers both have an emotional response to money. If you are doing it right, you should spend less than 1% of your time thinking about money, and there should be no positive or negative emotions associated with it. It simply is what it is.

I am a reformed CF. Boy did I used to be a CF—right until age 38, the day I bought those Prada boots. And yes, being frugal and investing wisely got me to a $200,000 net worth at age 27, when most of my peers were falling behind on student loans. When I was at Lehman Brothers—making that $850,000 a year—I was bringing in 69 cent cans of Beefaroni to lunch. People thought I was nuts. That was nuts. I thought everyone else was nuts, ordering in lunch all the time. I drove a Toyota Tercel up until 2003, at which point I splurged on a Toyota Camry. Let me put it this way—I was living *far* below my means.

And again, we look at these people who are living far above their means, and we say: "Those people are bad, those are the bad guys, with their BMWs and fancy clothes and luxury watches and whatever." But apparently we don't have a problem with someone who is making $850,000 a year who is living in a 1,600-square-foot house and driving a Toyota. We say that person is "down to earth." We say that person is grounded. You know what? Being down to earth is highly overrated. To me, it is a moral imperative—if you have means, you should enjoy the occasional luxury. Otherwise, what is the point of the money?

There is an answer here, and I actually stumbled upon it in my own journey. The thing about being a CF is that you're hard-wired to be a CF, and it's very difficult to change. The thing about being a high roller is that you're hard-wired to be a high roller, and it's very difficult to change. But you actually have to be both—at different times in your life. You have to be a CF at the beginning of your adult life, saving and investing early, because it is easier to forgo luxuries when you are younger. I lived in a 350-square-foot apartment out of college and it didn't bother me a bit. But then after age 45, when you have accumulated some wealth, it is time to spend it and enjoy the fruits of your labor.

But people find this very difficult to do. Once a CF, always a CF. Once a high roller, always a high roller. You must learn to be both.

Accumulate, then spend

I've been both. I've stayed in $15 hotel rooms when I was in my 20s—and $1,500 hotel rooms in my 40s. I've owned $15,000 cars and $115,000 cars. I've gotten my clothes at thrift stores and at some of the most expensive boutiques in the world. I waltzed into the Brioni store on Rodeo Drive and bought a $600 shirt—and that was early in my high roller days. You're supposed to save and invest for the future—and then when the future comes, you actually have to spend it. But most people never get to the second part—they are in accumulation mode their entire lives, while after age 45, they should be in decumulation mode.

This should be obvious, but maybe it isn't. You should spend the first part of your life accumulating assets—staking up big piles of cash—and the second half of your life *decumulating assets.* Spending that cash to buy stuff that brings you enjoyment. This is called delayed gratification. You work your ass off in your 20s and 30s so you can sit back in your 40s and 50s and buy overpriced shirts. This is what the high rollers get wrong— they spend early in life, and they are stuck later in life, and the reason this is a problem is that it is very hard to live a life of asceticism in your 50s and 60s. Much easier to do when you are younger. The high rollers don't know how to practice delayed gratification—they want gratification now.

The one thing all financially successful people have in common is delayed gratification—the ability to put off some pleasure today for more pleasure tomorrow. But sometimes we take delayed gratification too far—we never get to the gratification part. The dude that is living in his 1,200-square-foot house with the seven-figure bank account will die with that seven-figure bank account and never derive any enjoyment from his money.

A lot of that comes from fear—it could all go wrong at any moment. Sure, lots of things could go wrong—the stock market could crash, we could have a war, or even a pandemic, or maybe you just are afraid of losing your job—but all the psychological doomsday prepping that people do is completely unproductive. Most of the time, nothing bad happens. And by the way, I have never—not once in my life—regretted buying something because something bad happened later. You spend your whole life fearing the worst, and you miss out on the best.

It's good to have a healthy fear of the future. It's good to exercise some caution. But you can't be completely risk-averse.

And spending money is an act of self-affirmation—when you get enough money in the bank, and you're thinking about buying that house, it requires you to say: *I am worth it.* CFs typically have big self-esteem issues—they really don't think they are worth the house. But high rollers have self-esteem issues, too. They think they are worth the house, when they are in fact not. Getting this correct is a matter of being right-sized—not thinking too much of yourself, and not thinking too little of yourself.

Part of this is just math. If you have $15 million, you can buy the $2 million house, seven times over. If you have $0, you can't buy it, unless your income is very high. If you're thinking about making a major purchase, make sure the math checks out. We will discuss this later in the book.

If you're not a CF, then you're probably going to give more to charity. Americans donate more to charity than residents of any other country, but it's still not much. The median donation for *all* taxpayers, high-income and low-income, is $850. The typical household gives about 4% to charity, although we feel pretty smug every four years when presidential candidates release their tax returns and give "only" 10% to charity. Of course, the conventional wisdom is that you should give 10% to charity.

10% is a lot. I can say *for sure* that in my early years of accumulating assets, I never, ever got close to 10%. Because I was a CF. I would donate $1,000 to my high school and $1,000 to my college and call it a day. When I was making high six figures in income. That's a tragedy. I do think it makes sense to give a little less in your early years, and a little more in your later years, so you can invest that money and have it compound, resulting in more money given overall. I'm still not at my goal of giving 10% yet, but I'm giving 25 times what I was before. And the reason I am able to do this is because I have a healthy relationship with money; and when you don't live in fear of running out of money, or buried under debt service payments from consuming too much, you can give freely from a place of security and generosity. Put your mask on first, so you'll be able to assist others.

And it's not like high rollers are terribly generous, either—they're too busy falling behind on credit card bills to take out their checkbook and donate to a worthy cause. Free spending doesn't mean generous, most of the time. Again, it's impossible to sell a middle-ground solution, but that's what I'm trying to do—having a healthy relationship with money has benefits beyond your peace and happiness. It means that you have more space in your heart to help others in need. Giving hurts the CF, because he can't let the money go. Giving hurts the high roller, because he's living on the edge and behind on his payments. Balance is what is needed in your financial affairs.

I have known my share of CFs and high rollers over the years. More of the former than the latter. Multi-multi-millionaires who live in cheap houses, drive used cars, and shop for clothes at discount stores. I knew some high rollers in the mid-2000s with luxury apartments and wine fridges who lost everything in the Great Financial Crisis and had to start over again, from zero. I have seen shocking examples of both. People who have twisted relationships with money. Quite frankly, I'm ashamed of my CF past. And it's cost me money—by buying (much) smaller houses than I was able to afford, I haven't participated as much in real estate price appreciation. More simply, I would have been better off if I had bought bigger houses.

But I've always had a fear of debt. It's good to have a healthy respect for debt, because if you have too much debt, you're paying too much in interest, and it crowds out your ability to save for retirement. Debt is the only thing that can take you to zero—if you own your house and your car, and you have no other debt, such as student loans, nothing can touch you. You are financially invincible.

The correct use
of debt

Lots of people do use debt, with great care, and it all works out in the end. Out of all the people who take out 30-year fixed mortgages, oftentimes on houses they can't afford, very few of those loans go into default. The one thing I like about debt is that is an expression of optimism: "Everything's going to work out in the end." The pessimist CFs worry about recessions and crashes and big exogenous factors, and really don't believe that everything is going to work out in the end. And they miss out on a lot of life.

I currently don't have any debt—of any kind—and I can say that it is the greatest feeling in the world. If I say something stupid on Twitter and get canceled and lose my livelihood, I still have a house that is paid for, and I still have money in the bank. I am in an unassailable financial position.

But debt allows you to accomplish things you wouldn't have been able to otherwise. Take a walk down Madison Avenue in New York City. Look up at all the tall buildings. I assure you that those buildings were not paid for with cash. Every single one of them used copious amounts of debt—and everything worked out fine in the end. Go to places in the world where there is no debt, as the payment of interest is considered immoral. Not too many tall buildings, there. Not someplace I would want to live.

I don't want to get too much into debt—we will talk about that later—but I want to talk about the attitudes *surrounding* debt. Debt is risk. Things can go wrong. You can look at your situation optimistically, that nothing will go wrong, or, even if it does, you will be able to figure it out; or you can look at it pessimistically, and say, "Something is probably going to go wrong, and then I'll be screwed."

I prefer a course of qualified optimism, and I think it's important to be able to do the math. You're going to buy a house, the mortgage, insurance, and property taxes are x, which represents y percent of your income, and if you lose your job for whatever reason, you'll have enough in savings to make payments for z years, by which point you should have been able to find another job. If you can do the math, and you can get comfortable with the risk, then you can buy the house. What you don't want to do is *fall in love with the house*, start picturing all your kids and dogs and possessions in it, and then make an emotional decision on the house, which will cost you later.

The fear of recession

I want to talk a bit about recessions—the thing that everyone fears. A recession is a contraction in economic activity—it is when the economy shrinks for a period of time, rather than growing. When the economy contracts, people typically lose their jobs. In the Great Financial Crisis, the unemployment rate got up to 10%—millions of people lost their jobs. Even in 2020, during the coronavirus panic, unemployment got up to 11%, but then made a quick recovery. If we have a recession, it is very possible that you could lose your job—unless you work for the government, of course.

Capitalist economies have economic cycles. The economy grows for a number of years, and then shrinks for a couple of years. Expansion, and contraction. Two steps forward, one step back. For reasons that are a bit too complicated to explain here, we now get recessions very infrequently—one every ten years or so—but when they happen, they are deeper and more painful. And when it comes to the labor markets, people might find themselves out of a job for a year, two years, or more. And apart from losing your job, if you have a business, your revenues will likely decline as economic activity contracts. It is difficult to escape.

With all the financial technology in the world, we still don't have the ability to predict recessions. And we probably never will. But you do have some general idea of where you are in the cycle. If you were looking at real estate in 2010, you could be fairly certain that was the bottom of the cycle. If you were looking at real estate in 2021, you could be fairly certain that you were *not* at the bottom of the cycle—though you have no idea when a recession will begin. CFs survive recessions. High rollers sometimes don't. But in expansions, it is the high rollers who make money, while the CFs are left behind. This is why I don't do a lot of moralizing about high rollers. There are costs and benefits to both.

The typical wisdom on emergency funds is that you should have six months of expenses on hand, or $10,000, whichever is greater. You should probably have more than that, given that economic cycles are longer and deeper. A couple years should suffice. And you want to put away money in the good times, so you're not starving in the bad times—like that fable about the grasshopper and the ant. You want to be able to take enough risk so that you can thrive in economic expansions—and you want to save enough so that you can ride out recessions. Again, a middle-ground solution.

But recessions are not the end of the world. It feels like it, while you're going through it, but recessions often present huge opportunities for people with the 3 Cs—capital, conviction, and courage. At the bottom of the Great Financial Crisis, there were gigantic opportunities in real estate, stocks, and other assets. Most people didn't realize it at the time, because unemployment was roofing and people were in panic mode. But stuff was trading at a deep discount; and if you had capital, conviction, and courage, you could take advantage of these opportunities.

CFs are pretty good about having capital at the bottom of a recession—but they are too apprehensive to take advantage of low prices. High rollers can usually recognize the opportunities, but their capital is depleted and they are simply unable to act on these opportunities. For the millionth time, a middle-ground solution is best: be just cautious enough to build up savings in good times, so you can pounce on undervalued assets in bad times. Remember, in recession, it's not just houses that are cheap. They're giving cars away, and you can go to Best Buy and buy the whole store. Everything is on sale.

The CFs think they have it all figured out, and it is the rest of the world that is wrong. So do the high rollers. In each case, there is some very malignant psychology at play; the reason that people have bad relationships with money is usually because of some financial trauma in childhood. A profligate parent loses their job, and the family ends up on public assistance. A parent is too cheap to pay for college, and the child ends up going to a state school. I've found that it tends to be mean reverting across generations—if the parents are CFs, the children will become high rollers, and vice versa. You don't need a psychology PhD to figure that out.

Being too cheap or too spendthrift is actually a form of mental illness, and the problem is that we're holding up one variety of mental illness as the ideal, and telling people that's what they should strive for. The whole thing makes me mad. Just chill out and be smart.

Whether you like money, or dislike it, having an unhealthy relationship with money will not only make you miserable, but everyone around you as well. In the next chapter, we talk about *relationships and money.*

....

CHAPTER 6

Relationships
and Money

What is the most important personal finance decision you will make in your life?

It is not what stock to buy, or what mutual fund to invest in.

It is not whether you get a 15- or 30-year mortgage.

It is not whether you should use the snowball method to pay down your credit cards.

The most important personal finance decision you will make in your life is:

Who to marry.

When selecting a partner, you want to choose someone who shares your values on money. More succinctly, CFs can't marry high rollers, and vice versa. It just won't work out.

Not only will it not work out, but it's going to blow up like a supernova.

This is real. Marriages end because of money. All the time. I've heard stories about people getting into screaming matches over some inconsequential amount of money, like $50. Man. That is not the way to live.

If you're a high roller husband and you go and buy a $90 T-shirt, your CF wife is going to freak out. And you're going to have a resentment because you can't buy the T-shirt you really want. Multiply this by a million economic decisions over the course of a marriage. You see where I am going with this.

Most people operate under the assumption that when they get married, they will combine every aspect of their lives, including their financial lives. Some people say that a marriage is not consummated until the couple gets a joint bank account: "We no longer have my money and your money; we have *our* money. We're a team, and if we're making decisions together as a couple, then we should combine our resources." Reasonable enough.

Except the problem is that the individuals in a marriage never really stop keeping track of whose money is whose. It's in the joint account, but everyone knows what they contributed, so the husband still thinks the wife is spending his money, or the wife still thinks that the husband is spending her money. We can't get rid of these emotional attachments. So the best solution to this, believe it or not, is:

Keep your money separate.

My story

I will tell you my story.

I got married at a very young age—23—and I was a huge

CF, and the nice thing was that I found a partner who was an even bigger CF. She grew up even poorer than I did. I got my CF ways from living in Connecticut—the land of nutmeggers with LL Bean sweaters who break out the 18% tip calculator when they go out to dinner. For a while, my wife's family was subsisting on $3,000 a year—her dad was a taxidermist, and not a very commercially successful one. Most of the food came from hunting or the vegetable garden.

My wife and I were CFs extraordinaire. When we moved to a small town in Washington State, we found the cheapest apartment possible.

As soon as we got married, we had the discussion. How are we going to handle our money? We both agreed that the best course of action was to keep our money separate—forever. My money is my money, and her money is her money. That way there will be no fights about money. If I want to buy stuff, there is nothing she can say about it; and if she wants to buy stuff, there is nothing I can say about it.

Now, of course, we had common expenses. We had to pay the rent. The rent was $350 a month. So we agreed that we would pay proportionally relative to our respective incomes. I ended up paying about $160 a month and she ended up paying about $190 a month, as she was making more money than me at the time. We split the utility bill in the same fashion.

As for food, we agreed that I would pay two-thirds of the grocery bill, because I ate two-thirds of the food. We would each pay our own car insurance. Everything else we split 50/50.

What about the mortgage? We bought our first house in 1999, after we had just turned 25. I don't remember what the mortgage payment was, but I'm guessing it was around $1,500 a month. Interest rates were about 7% at the time.

We contributed to the mortgage proportionally, just like we did with rent—although at the time she wasn't working, and going to grad school, so she was contributing only a nominal amount out of her savings. I built a spreadsheet in Microsoft Excel, constructing an amortization table for the mortgage, keeping track of the principal that each of us paid. I added up all our equity in the house, combining our principal payments with the down payment (which we split 50/50), and determined our percentage ownership. By the time we sold it, I owned about 53% of the house, and she owned about 47% of the house, and I got 53% of the cash, and she got 47%.

This was done for the sake of our marriage—and eliminating arguments. In our current house, I own about 87%, and she owns 13%. When we sell this house and roll the proceeds into the next one, we will do the same thing: build the spreadsheet and keep track of our equity contribution.

At this point some wise guy is probably saying, "What happens if you get divorced? She's going to get half anyway." Perhaps. The handshake agreement that we have is that if we part amicably, we will go our separate ways with the money we have, and if we don't (in the case of infidelity or something else), then the lawyers are going to get involved and she's going to get half.

This may sound like a very complicated system (and it is), but let me tell you—we have been married for 26 years, *and we have only fought about one aspect of money, ever—and that is taxes.*

You see, even though we keep our money separate, we file taxes jointly because it makes economic sense—we pay less money. My wife gets taxes withheld from her paycheck (she is a W-2 employee) and I pay estimated taxes for my business. At the end of the year, we have a combined effective tax rate.

For a while, my wife was making the argument that she should be taxed at a lower rate because she has less income. But I made the argument that we both enjoy a higher standard of living because of my income; and besides, if she paid less taxes, it would mean that I would have to pay even more in taxes—

sometimes over 40%. For a few years, I went into the tax tables and figured out her tax liability corresponding with her lower income, but this got to be a pain and I got sick of writing checks for a few thousand bucks to her every year.

We still don't have an answer for this, though I think my way is the right way, and it is getting to the point where I earn about 95% of the income, so it's almost a moot point. This is the *only* time we have ever fought about money—and the fights weren't even that bad.

We have fought about other things, for sure, but we don't fight about money. And that's important! Because fighting about money is stupid, and money arguments just compound all the other arguments, and make things worse. There are plenty of things to worry about in a marriage and money should not be one of them.

It helps that we have the same values when it comes to money. It's good that we keep our money separate, but the marriage would still be difficult if one of us was a high roller and the other was a CF. And by the way, I probably make it seem like this only works one way—that CFs should not marry high rollers, because they will overspend and go into debt. But high rollers should not marry CFs either, because they'll find them to be boring buzzkills. You want someone that shares your values on money—even if they are not great values.

The big decisions you have to make together

Another important point is that my wife always had a role in the household finances. Because she was paying, she knew where the money was going. She also knows the existence and location of all my accounts, and I know the existence and location of all her accounts.

This isn't one of those marriages where one person handles the money, and the other is completely in the dark. That's bad news. This is how people get trapped in abusive relationships, and they can't leave. This isn't just about agency—this is about safety. It may be tempting to remain ignorant of financial matters—"Oh, my husband handles all the money stuff"—but it will cost you in the end. Everyone is responsible for their own financial education.

Which is a point I want to emphasize a bit more—you see, we don't teach finance in schools, although that is starting to change, as some states are adding personal finance to their high-school curricula. But for the most part, we aren't taught about money—we are left to figure it out for ourselves. Some people do a good job at that—and some people do not. It is completely self-directed.

There are a lot of consequences to this, and one of the biggest is that financially illiterate people are highly susceptible to fraud. But more commonly, they do things like get ripped off for a couple of thousand bucks at car dealerships. Being financially illiterate has a cost, and it is not small. It is as important as being able to read and write. And both partners in a relationship should have some degree of financial literacy.

You're in this together. You're a team. And just because you have shared goals, it doesn't mean you need to combine your finances. My wife and I have always had shared goals. Five houses, seven cars, three stints in grad school, and we have been able to accomplish this without establishing one single joint account.

Remember, working as team, you have to get the big decisions right—the house, the car, and the student loans.

Buying a house is, hands down, the most important big financial decision you will make in your life. And it is a decision that must be made together. I'll go into more detail into houses and mortgages in Chapter 9, but I do want to examine the decision-making process when a couple picks out a dwelling.

What should be a coldly rational financial decision becomes an emotional decision. Most commonly, a couple falls in love with a house, has visions of raising a family there, in a nice neighborhood, with great schools, but there's a problem: the house is a bit more than they can afford. In any marriage there is usually one left-brain person that crunches the numbers, and one right-brain person that, well, carries the emotional burden. It is rarely the left-brain person that wins these arguments. Buying too big of a house, and having too much debt, can be crippling. It can crowd out your ability to save for retirement, and for fun things, like vacations. Do the math. Figure out your monthly income, after tax, then figure out your mortgage, insurance, and property taxes. You should not be spending more than 25% of your income on housing costs.

Money relationships with family and friends

Relationships and money don't just have to do with married couples—they involve parents and children, brothers and sisters, and friends. And the one thing I want to focus on is lending money to family and friends.

Simple enough: don't do it. It will ruin the relationship. Here's why.

Let's say your brother-in-law approaches you to borrow

$25,000 for his tractor business. You have a choice. Lend him the money, or don't lend him the money. If you don't lend him the money, he won't like it very much, and he'll move onto someone else. If you do lend him the money, either he will pay you back—crisis averted—or he won't, and then it's going to be awkward. You will be blowing up his phone to get your money back. And he knows he owes you the money, so he will be dodging your calls. At this point, the relationship is ruined. Actually, it was ruined *at the point he asked you for the money*. But not lending him the money, and having him be mad at you, is the better outcome.

If someone wants to borrow money, they have these things called banks, you know. At the bank there are tellers and computers and offices, and it feels very much like you are borrowing money. They do credit checks; you have to sign all this paperwork. It's a very formal process. There is a purpose to this: the bank wants to keep this as impersonal as possible, because if it goes wrong, and they need to foreclose on you, there will be no hesitation.

But if your brother-in-law comes to *you* to borrow money, it means one of two things: either he doesn't want to go through this formal process, because he knows there is a likelihood he will default, and unlike the bank, he knows you have no legal recourse. Or, his credit is so impaired that no bank will lend to him and he has exhausted all other possibilities. Either scenario is bad for you, the lender. The answer to the question, "Can I borrow $25,000?" is always, always no.

Unless...

Unless the relationship is important to you, or saying no will cause some ugly family dynamics, or whatever dumb reason you have—and I assure you, it is dumb; but let's say you have decided to lend $25,000 to your brother-in-law's failing tractor business—you want to think of it as a gift. As soon as you write the check, you assume that money is gone and you will never see it again. You write it to zero. If you get paid back, it is a bonus.

The best way to structure this is as a forgivable loan with an infinite term: "Pay me back when you can." There is a reason you do this: if your brother-in-law knows that he owes you money, and he hasn't paid you back, it is very unlikely that he will ask you for more money.

Or the alternative is that you can get a lawyer involved and write up a loan agreement and charge your brother-in-law interest. And it should probably be a lot of interest, because remember, your brother-in-law has exhausted all other possibilities, and no other creditor will lend to him. So you could do that. But I doubt your brother-in-law will agree to it.

The important thing is to treat it as a gift in your mind, because if you don't, you will develop a resentment against your brother-in-law, and it will consume you. And remember what they say about resentment: resentment is like drinking poison and waiting for the other person to die. This is to preserve your mental health, not his.

It's possible that at some point in your life, you will have a friend or a family member who will want you to invest in their business. You have to evaluate this critically, because sometimes the family member is smart and hardworking and has a really good idea, and you think he can execute on that idea. You should evaluate opportunities like these based on merit. The business idea may sound attractive; but out of a range of other possible business ideas you haven't heard of, is this the one you would choose?

I have heard one story of a family investment going *very* well, resulting in millions of dollars. A good friend of mine invested $25,000 in an exercise bike company that turned into $9 million when it went public. That company was Peloton.

Early-stage investing can be one of the most profitable things you can do—with virtually unlimited upside—but it should not make up more than 10% of your total net worth.

Most early-stage ventures fail, a few of them do ok, and once in a great while, it will turn into a home run. Investing in young companies is a good way of getting *upside*, which we talked about before. But the failing tractor business is probably not a good idea.

The key principle here is business first, friends second, not the other way around. If you're friends first, and do business second, you're likely not going to be friends at the end of it.

Teaching kids about money

When it comes to parents and children, there are a host of competing philosophies on how you should teach your kids about money. Most parents give allowances, which vary in size. This is commonplace. Other parents don't give allowances at all, and instead pay the child for completing tasks around the house, treating the child as an employee of a business. Others do a combination of the two. I got an allowance of $10 a week, and earned extra money by washing cars or shoveling snow.

Most people think of an allowance as a salary. You can dock the kid's pay for bad behavior. There really are no wrong answers here, except in situations where children learn that there are no constraints on money. Wealthy families have the ability to satisfy all of the child's needs and wants, and frequently do—and as a result, children do not learn the value of money. I was raised by my mother and grandmother, and my grandmother used to give me two quarters to play video games while she drank coffee in the diner. I never got more than two. Consequently, I got really good at playing video games.

The biggest financial question a parent will face when raising children is: who will pay for college? Some parents consider it their responsibility, and theirs alone, to pay for higher education. Other parents want the child to share in that responsibility. Other parents refuse to pay for college altogether.

I tend to be a bit more progressive in my thinking about this: parents should shoulder all or most of the burden of paying for college. There are decisions to be made about what college to pay for: the $80,000-a-year private liberal arts college may not be a great value. But I believe that parents should be responsible for providing a baseline college education to each of their children, if that is what they desire. I can tell you, though, that if the child has his or her heart set on a particular school, and the parents refuse to pay for it, this is going to create a resentment that could last for decades.

The reality is that name-brand schools, like the Ivies, provide all sorts of tangible and intangible benefits, and almost always result in better employment prospects, with higher pay. It may be tempting to take the cheaper option with a state school, perhaps in an honors program, but that is the hard way, not the easy way. Prestigious schools typically admit wealthy students with connections that will bear fruit for years.

Should a parent buy a car for their teenage child? Opinions differ. I was saved from this decision when my grandmother passed away shortly before I turned 15. When I turned 16, I inherited the car, and my mother paid the insurance. It was a brown Pontiac 1000 of the 1986 vintage, which was basically a Chevette. I had a job at the time (as a church organist), but I was only making enough money to cover the gas, and not the insurance. I was grateful for the help.

In the 1980s, it would have been possible for a teenager to buy a used car for as little as $500, but that's not realistic today, as new and used cars are much more expensive. I don't think it's bad parenting to purchase a car for the kid, and perhaps a better arrangement is where the child shares in the burden in some small proportion.

I'm sure you've heard that not as many teenagers have jobs these days, and that is too bad. Teenagers should have jobs, no matter how stultifying. The last thing you want is for your child's first day of work to be when they are 22. The skills that a teenager acquires at a part-time job are not the skills you think they acquire—nobody aspires to be a burger-flipper later in life. But showing up on time, in the right clothes, ready to work, and putting forth maximum effort is what should be learned at age 16, not age 22.

....

Most people do not think of the effect that their money habits have on relationships. Being a CF can *really* harm relationships. Your kids will one day tell their therapist that their father refused to pay for college. So can being a high roller. Your spouse will be creating secret accounts and hiding money so you can't spend it. The goal here is to have a healthy relationship with money—to earn it well, treat it with respect, spend judiciously, and invest the rest. People are watching you—and will imitate your actions.

We should all strive to achieve balance in our financial lives, and to have a *healthy relationship with money*. We shouldn't love it too much or too little. Not just for our sake, but for those around us.

In the next section, we will be getting into the weeds on debt—specific kinds of debt. These will be the building blocks for your new financial life.

PART III

Debt
Stress

CHAPTER 7

....

The Power of Cash

Why we have money

Let's say we have an economy that consists of two people: me and you. I write financial newsletters and you make nozzles. I write a newsletter and I walk down the street to your house, because I need a nozzle. This is called barter. We're going to trade newsletters for nozzles.

But maybe you don't want a newsletter—maybe you want something else. Maybe you want chicken. So you would take my newsletter and give me a nozzle, and then hope to trade either a nozzle or a newsletter for some chicken.

Barter doesn't work very well. This is why we have money.
This is how it works. When I write a newsletter, I create
value, which I trade for *money*. I can then use the money to
trade for something else I want—literally anything, because
everyone else creates nozzles or chicken and trades it for money.

Money is a unit of account—it's how we measure value. It's
a store of value—I can keep the money in my house for an
indefinite period of time and then I can buy stuff with it later.
It's also a medium of exchange—everyone accepts it universally.

We're beginning this part on debt stress with a discussion
about cash because in order to understand how debt works,
you first need to understand how *money* works.

Keeping cash
in the bank

Once we've accumulated a big pile of money, our house is not
a very convenient place to have it. Someone could break in and
take it. Wouldn't it be nice if there was a safe place to put it?

Enter the bank. A bank is a safe place to put your money.

The crazy thing about banks is that they used to pay you
for the privilege of storing your money there, which is kind of
counterintuitive. Then we had a long period of zero percent
interest rates. You put your money in the bank and you might
get $2 of interest all year. If banks paid more in interest, then
people might keep more money in the bank and less in the
stock market, but that is a longer discussion.

You may find this hard to believe, but in the not-so-distant
past, interest rates were high enough that putting money in a
bank was a real investment strategy. If you could get 8% a year

on your money in the bank—a sure thing—there is no reason to look at stocks.

Even today, keeping your money in the bank is still not the worst idea in the world. The nice thing about having money in the bank is that you can't lose it, which is a very underrated property of money in the bank. Money in a bank account is FDIC insured for up to $250,000.

Most people are terrible investors. JP Morgan did a study of investment returns between 1999 and 2019. Over that time period, stocks returned 5.6% annually, but the average investor returned about 1.9%—worse than bonds. And if the average investor is making 1.9%, that means that a certain number of investors—say, 30% of them—are actually earning negative returns in the context of a big bull market in stocks. Which is another way of saying that they lost money, even though stocks were going up. Isn't that nuts?

This one-third of people will never need to invest in the stock market. And there is a good chance that you are one of the 30%. Cash in a bank account is just fine. Why? Because making zero percent in the bank is better than making negative percent in the stock market.

Everyone was really excited between 2011 and 2021, and investing in the stock market seemed so easy; but I assure you, there will come a point in time when it is not so easy. When I was doing my radio show, the number one question I would get would be: "How do I invest in the stock market?" I would get this question from Uber drivers with $2,000 in savings. I would respond, "There are some other things you need to do first."

The returns that people see on the stock indexes, like the Dow, or the S&P 500, are illusory—*unless you do everything right*. Unless you dollar cost average perfectly and never sell. From an evolutionary perspective, human beings are hard-wired to be bad investors. I am no different. We will find a way to lose money. So making zero in the bank is not the worst thing in the world. With one caveat: Inflation.

In periods of high inflation, it makes less sense to keep money in the bank. At the time of writing, in 2023, we are experiencing a period of high inflation. This makes keeping money in the bank a very unattractive proposition. The math behind this is as follows: if you have 6% inflation, and you are making zero percent in the bank, then it is like you are making negative 6% on your money.

But there are *still* lots of reasons why you want to do keep money in the bank.

The emergency fund

The first reason you want to have cash is for *emergency funds*. This is a very important rule that you *must follow*: keep six to 12 months' worth of expenses *in the bank* in case of emergencies. Because you just never know.

So let's say your rent is $2,000 a month and your cell phone and utilities and everything else is a few hundred dollars a month, and your food is about $500 a month, and you add up all your expenses, and it comes out to about $4,000 a month. That's $48,000 a year. That means you must have $24,000 in emergency funds *in the bank, in your checking account*, at a minimum—at all times. Preferably you'd have up to $48,000.

What is the reasoning here?

Well, if the worst happens, and you lose your job, you could safely live off your emergency funds for a period of six to 12 months before you found another job. And you'll be getting unemployment benefits simultaneously, so you can last even longer.

Remember, this is about living a stress-free financial life. Imagine you get to a point where *nothing can touch you*—you lose your job, no big deal. Car transmission breaks, no big deal. Your cat gets sick, no big deal. That's what the money is for.

The last one is a big one for me—I'm an animal lover, and literally millions of pets are euthanized every year because their owners don't have the money for some lifesaving medical treatment. It's called economic euthanasia. Don't be one of those people. Plan ahead. It's why I could never be a vet—someone comes in and can't afford $500 to take care of their cat. *All* of this misery can be prevented by having an emergency fund.

Don't get cheap about the emergency fund—like, you don't want to spend the $500. As soon as you deposit money in the emergency fund (create a separate account if necessary), think of it as spent. That's an insurance policy. The money is there to cover unforeseen expenses.

And for the love of God, don't invest the emergency funds. It doesn't matter that you're getting paid zero interest, that you're losing money with inflation—just leave it in the checking account. I've heard of people investing their emergency funds in crypto. Insanity.

Build up your emergency funds before you do *anything else*. Before you buy a house, before you buy a car, before you buy stocks, before you buy crypto. If that seems like a lot of money to invest in an emergency fund, it's not. I assure you that my emergency fund is much larger than that. But my emergency fund is not just for emergencies; it's for other stuff too.

Which brings us to the option value of cash.

The option value
of cash

Cash is a big pile of options. You have $50,000 in your bank account. It's just sitting there, not doing anything. But it could be doing something. What could you be doing with it?

Well, a good investment opportunity might come along. Or maybe you are traveling and you come across your dream house. Or a vintage car that you've always wanted is listed online. Whether it's investment or consumption, you want cash to take advantage of these opportunities. You can't do any of these things unless you have cash.

The house I am currently living in (which I bought in 2015) was made possible by a sizable cash balance in my bank account. I simply wrote the check for the down payment, and there was none of this brain damage around selling stocks or taking out second loans to pay for this thing. Just write a check—done.

This may seem like a foreign concept to you, but you will get opportunities like this in your lifetime. Whether it's a stock, or a brother-in-law's business, or a hedge fund, or even something fun to buy, there will be numerous times in your life when these opportunities come around. And you have to be ready for them, by having lots of cash on hand.

Ultimately, I recommend that 20% of your net worth is held in cash, for emergencies, to take advantage of opportunities, or for portfolio reasons, which we will discuss in Part IV.

This is about living a stress-free financial life. Having a large cash cushion dramatically reduces your financial stress.

One of my favorite movies of all time is the 2014 remake of *The Gambler*, starring Mark Wahlberg. John Goodman plays a loan shark, and gives the best speech about money I have ever seen in a movie. The speech is expletive-laden and essentially says that once you have no debt and a big pile of cash, you are indestructible. This is said to be reaching a position of "F★★★ you." No description can do it justice—you have to see the movie. It might be Mark Wahlberg's worst performance, but the movie is still outstanding.

Having a huge cash position is dealing from a position of power.

Here's what happens if you have a huge portfolio of stocks. First scenario: they go up, and you don't want to sell them. Second scenario: they go down, and you don't want to sell them. No matter what, you are not going to want to sell your stocks. Because you like them—you think they're good investments. So you're asset rich, and cash poor.

Having a bunch of assets makes you very fragile. Having a large cash position reduces your fragility. It makes you indestructible, actually.

Of course, there are trade-offs. There are trade-offs between returns and safety. I place a higher value on safety than I do on returns. Remember, the goal is not to be a millionaire; the goal is to live a stress-free financial life.

So many people refuse to keep cash in the bank because they think they are "missing out" on gains in the stock market. They say, "My money isn't working for me."

Wrong.

Let the cash sit there in the bank: it is serving a purpose, and that purpose is your mental health. There is nothing else that is more important.

Liquidity

Let's have a discussion about liquidity.

Liquidity is the property where an asset can easily be turned into cash. Cash is the definition of liquidity—it is already cash. Most stocks are liquid—they are not so hard to sell, although there are some stocks that are thinly traded that take some time to get out of if you have a large position. Mutual funds, both stock and bond, are liquid—mutual fund companies are required by law to meet redemption orders.

Real estate is not so liquid. If you have a house, and you want to sell it, it will take three months. Not a good thing if you want to take your money out in a hurry. That's the main problem I have with real estate investing—if you have ten to 12 houses that you are renting out, if you wanted to sell them, it would take a year, and if a recession hits in the meantime, you are going down for the dirtnap.

Likewise, stock in private corporations is also not liquid. You are probably holding it until some kind of liquidity event, like an acquisition, or an IPO, or something like that. If you have the opportunity to invest in private businesses, know that your capital is going to be locked up for a long period of time.

Living a stress-free financial life means maintaining a strong liquidity position at all times. If you are a real estate investor, and you have ten to 12 houses, you will want to have a lot of cash on hand. Don't be one of these asset-rich/cash-poor people. This is how you get into trouble. Unfortunately, a lot of people live this way.

If you have cash, you have the *liquidity* to handle emergencies, you have the *liquidity* to make investments at opportune times, and you have the *liquidity* to spend your time how you want to. Cash is highly, highly underrated.

Keeping money in cash

The question is: where do you keep your cash? In the bank? Somewhere else?

The answer might surprise you. I think that a decent amount of your cash should be kept in *actual cash*, like paper currency.

Let me give you an example. A storm blows through and knocks a tree on your roof. It also knocks the power out. How will you get the tree off your roof? If you call the tree guy, how will you pay him, if credit cards don't work? And even if they do work, the tree guy is more likely to help you out first if you can hand him $5,000 in cash.

I've never been able to figure out the people who go to the ATM to get $40. They'll use it up in two days, and be back at the ATM. People have an unfounded fear of getting robbed. For sure, there are places where you don't want $500 in your wallet. But otherwise, the chance of getting robbed is microscopic; and if you do get robbed, you've got bigger things to worry about than $500. There is also the chance that you lose your wallet, I suppose, and you'd be upset if there was a lot of cash in there. But the cash is frequently less of a concern than the huge hassle of having to cancel all your credit cards and stand in line at the DMV for a new license.

When I go to the ATM, I get $600, in $50 bills. It will last me for a few weeks. I try to pay for as many things as I can with cash, for a bunch of reasons. One is privacy—I'm not doing anything suspicious, but there doesn't need to be an electronic record of where I go to lunch every day.

But the bigger reason is that when you have a wallet full of cash, and you spend it over time, and you run out of cash—

that's it, you are out of cash. Not long ago someone came up with the idea of a cash diet, where you give up using credit cards for a few months or so, and only carry cash. That is a good way to keep track of how much money you're spending. Most people have no idea, when using credit cards, but once they blow through all the cash in their wallet or purse, they're out, and they're done spending for the month. I find tips and tricks like this to be gimmicky at times, but I'm all for the cash diet.

Also, I like to keep stuff off the credit card. I have money and a bunch of good habits around spending, but I'm uncomfortable with the idea that I might one day run up a big balance and be unable to pay it. It's just good practice to pay for stuff with cash. Plus, there have been a few instances in which people have given me a discount for paying in cash. A jewelry store did this.

If you calculate that you need about $24,000 in emergency funds, then it's not unreasonable to keep about $5,000 to $10,000 of that in cash at home. If you're nervous about it, get a safe. Or find a secret place to hide it.

All this aside, I've found that I've had some difficulty in getting cash out of the bank at times. Banks nowadays don't keep a lot of cash on hand, partially to deter robberies. I was at the bank one time and a guy came in to withdraw $7,000 in cash to pay a contractor that was working on his house. The bank wouldn't give it to him. The teller told him that they *did not have that much money in the bank*, which was probably a lie. They told him if he wanted $7,000, he had to order it a week in advance. The guy was totally hosed. I've found that I'm able to get increments of $3,000 out without incident. But they always ask me why I want the cash. I simply tell them, "I want money outside the financial system." That seems to shut them up.

You probably know that if you take out more than $10,000 at a time, a report gets filed with the government. Some people try to get around this by taking out $9,000 at a time, but don't do this—there's actually a law against that, too, and it's called structuring. The whole thing is a scam because the $10,000 limit was passed in the 1970s and hasn't been adjusted for inflation. If it was, it would be $70,000 today. Guess what: America is not a financially free country; but that is a subject for another book, perhaps.

Other places to keep cash

Where else are you supposed to keep cash? Well, the bank, obviously. It's safe, and it's insured. Problem is, it doesn't pay anything in interest. An alternative is money market mutual funds, but at the time of writing, the money market industry is a mess. The good news is that they are liquid.

If you want to earn some interest on your cash, there is the option of certificates of deposit (CDs), or high-yielding savings accounts. These days, they don't give you much in the way of interest, although that that seems to be in the process of changing. CDs, as you probably know, require you to lock up your money for a set amount of time in exchange for higher interest. I've actually never gotten a CD, because the main benefit of having cash in the bank is that it is immediately available. If you need to take your money out of a CD, then you have to pay a penalty. Like I said, the skinny yields on CDs and money market funds generally make them not worthwhile, but that began to change in 2022.

One not-well-known place to park cash is Treasury Direct—a government website that allows you to directly purchase U.S. Treasury bills and bonds. Most people use this to buy T-bills: securities with less than one year maturity. I don't know anyone who has bought a 30-year bond on Treasury Direct. But as recently as 2022, you could buy T-bills yielding 5% and up, which wasn't available at the bank. You can also buy I bonds—inflation-linked bonds—at Treasury Direct, which are super interesting at a time of high inflation; but you are restricted to $10,000 in purchases.

As for the poor EE savings bond, that ended up being perhaps the greatest example of government incompetence I've ever seen. Savings bonds were a great low-tech way for people to save money. You go to the bank and get a paper certificate, and put it in a file cabinet at home. Obama ended the savings program in favor of something called myRA, which was intended to be something like an IRA that invested in Treasury bills and bonds, but it was a complete bust, and Trump euthanized that program. Of all the ways for the government to look for ways to save money, cutting the savings bond program was the dumbest.

Gold

This is the point in the book where I reluctantly talk about gold.

It's hard to have a rational discussion about gold. Gold has *political* implications. If you own gold, it basically means you think the government is going to mess up, print too much money, and create inflation. If you don't, it's an expression of faith in the authorities doing the right thing. Right-wing people tend to like gold. Left-wing people don't. Some of the right-wing people get carried away and become *gold bugs*, and put substantially all their assets in gold, and then spend all their time reading gold newsletters and conspiracy theory websites. There is a nutball element to it, for sure. But gold has a place.

Lots of people are curious about whether they should have some exposure to gold. The problem is, if you're not rich, and you want to buy *physical* gold, the transaction costs get very high, and you're in fractional coin hell. But the good news is that there are cheap and easy ways to get exposure to gold without the hassle of buying coins and bars and storing them in your house.

In 2005, when I was head of ETF trading at Lehman Brothers, I was approached by a couple of guys from State Street and the World Gold Council. They wanted to start a gold ETF—a fund that was backed by physical gold in an underground vault in London. One share of GLD (the ticker) would be worth one-tenth of an ounce of gold. The fund had expenses of 0.4% per year, which was paid by the fund selling a little bit of gold out of the vault on the open market. To say that the launch was successful would be an understatement. Only the bitcoin futures ETF gathered more assets in such a short amount of time. Today, anyone has the ability to buy gold in securitized form.

The gold bugs are annoying purists who say that if you don't hold the gold directly, i.e. coins and bars in your house, then you really don't own gold. That's not the case. The reason you want to hold physical gold is for the unlikely scenario where the financial system collapses, and you have to buy pork chops with... gold coins? There are reasons to own gold other than as a hedge against the world coming to an end, which we will cover later in the book. A lot of people think of gold as *safety*, which it really is not. We'll discuss later.

....

Cash is very, very underrated. Most finance people have a dim view of cash. It's a drag on returns, they say. You want to be fully invested, they say. Easy to say when the market goes straight up for ten years.

Cash is an option to buy something cheaper in the future. And options are very, very valuable. Ask me about the time I bought a piece of land near the beach with cash I had laying around. Six months later, it had doubled in value. True story. Life is full of opportunities, if your eyes are open. And you need cash to take advantage of them.

With that said about the security and relief of stress offered by holding cash, we'll now move on the four areas of debt that cause stress, beginning with credit cards.

CHAPTER 8

Credit Cards Can Be Stressful

Living in the moment has its perks. One of my favorite sayings to myself is, "I don't have to decide this right now. I'll worry about that later."

The purpose of this is to reduce stress in the short term.

A few years ago, I bought a clock for my office (paid for with cash) that has the word *NOW* on it in big capital letters. It's to remind me that if we live in the past or the future, we'll be miserable—we're only happy if we live in the present.

But the purchasing decisions we make *NOW* have consequences that extend into the future. If you're using a credit card to pay for $200-worth of picture frames at Target, and you decide to worry about it later, then you *will* worry about it later. You don't get out of worrying about it by putting it on a credit card. The credit card postpones the worry to a later date, when the sum of all your postponed decisions is staring you in the face in the form of a big monthly bill.

NOW the real stress begins.

You must be very judicious about the types of things you put on a credit card. A credit card is a convenient way to pay for things, so you should use a credit card when convenience is necessary. You should not use a credit card for frivolous spending unless that purchase is *cash-secured*. Meaning you already have the money in your bank account.

An example: I am a fashion plate and I like to buy clothes from John Varvatos. I do not live near a John Varvatos store, so I buy their clothes online. With a credit card. Some of their clothes are expensive. I will only press the "buy" button if I have the cash in my bank account to pay for it outright. You do not want to be paying interest on discretionary purchases. You do not want to be paying interest at all (which we will discuss in a moment); but you especially don't want to be paying interest on discretionary stuff.

Like tattoos.

I have lots of tattoos and I love my tattoos. Every time I got a tattoo, I brought $2,000 in cash to the tattoo parlor. Every time. I do not put a tattoo on a credit card. Think to yourself, "What is the dumbest thing that I could pay interest on?" And a tattoo has to be pretty close to the top of the list.

I would much rather be paying interest on groceries, or something else essential, than tattoos or jackets from John Varvatos.

....

Some people say that credit cards are the root of all evil. I disagree.

I could be the guy that claims credit cards are evil, don't use credit cards, cut them up, and go off the grid and use cash all the time. That would definitely fix your credit card problem, but it makes life extraordinarily difficult. Let me put it this way: this is not a habit of highly effective people.

A responsible credit card user understands that building credit in the short term is an important part of paying for those big decisions—house, car, college—in the long term. You don't qualify for a mortgage by existing off the grid. It is very hard—nay, impossible—in the 21st century to get a hotel or a rental car without a credit card. You can't be part of civilized society these days without a convenient way to pay for things electronically.

But like with my tattoos, you need to decide where using a credit card makes financial sense. Credit cards, while useful, can cause a great deal of financial stress. Which may seem obvious, but it isn't obvious to everyone. If you've ever failed to pay the entire balance in a given month, there is a sense of impending doom as you submit that minimum payment—you know that this balance is going to get bigger and bigger over time.

And one of the reasons it gets bigger is because credit cards are a revolving debt, rather than an installment debt. A mortgage is an installment debt—you make a fixed payment each month, consisting of principal and interest. Whereas the interest on revolving debt gets calculated monthly, and after a while, interest is charged on top of interest, and it grows exponentially.

There is a quote that is probably falsely attributed to Einstein: "Compound interest is the eighth wonder of the world." Negative compounding interest is like scraping the back of your thighs with a cheese grater.

You want your money to *compound* a little bit each year, earning interest (or returns in the stock market), multiplying over time. If you're stuck in credit card-land, and your wealth is negatively compounding, abandon all hope ye who enter here. This only happens with credit card debt, not other kinds of debt, which is what makes it so dangerous.

I may come across as glib and avuncular when I say that credit cards are a convenient way to pay for things, but I don't want to undersell how pernicious they can be. All it takes is a little bit of inattention to get behind, and then you get behind on being behind.

How people view credit cards is different from how they view cash. If there were no such thing as credit cards, and you wanted to buy a $500 jacket, but you didn't have the cash, you couldn't buy it. If you don't have a *plan* to pay for the jacket when you're standing in the store, you shouldn't buy the jacket.

Credit cards are not free money. Pay now or pay later, eventually you will have to pay. And if that $500 stays on your balance long enough, you will end up paying the same amount again, or more, in interest. Yes, then you will have paid for the jacket several times over.

I imagine that our lives would be worse without credit cards. We'd all have to carry around huge amounts of cash. We'd be standing there at the grocery store checkout, counting change. Credit cards are a time-saving invention. But if used improperly, they can cause a great deal of misery.

....

Let's talk about how to use credit cards the right way.

Simple: pay off the balance every month.

Some things are easier said than done. This shouldn't be one of them. You need to reevaluate your relationship with credit cards if you desire any kind of stress relief.

Understand that credit cards are a convenient way to pay for things. But they are a profoundly bad way to borrow money.

"Easy for you to say, Dillian. I don't have the money to pay off the balance each month," you say. Well, there is an easy solution to that. Spend less. But you say you can't.

This is the point where you pull up a chair at your kitchen table and you make a budget. Research how much money you make on an after-tax basis, take out your credit card statements, chart out all your monthly expenses, and look for a shortfall. If you have a shortfall, the problem is not the credit card—it's the spending.

The credit card is allowing you to have a higher standard of living today at the expense of having a lower standard of living tomorrow.

This debt will catch up with you, and the only way around this is to cut expenses. It's not a credit card problem; it's a budgeting problem. The credit card allows you to believe that you don't actually have a problem. You'll spend the rest of your life financing this balance that keeps growing over time, until you get religion and pay it off, or you go bankrupt. Or you pay interest on the balance forever, and the interest adds up to tens of thousands of dollars over time. Money that you could have used for something more productive.

So how you do get out of this seemingly endless soul-sucking cycle of debt?

Pay off your balance
every month

It bears repeating, because people have a tough time doing this.

It used to be that there was no easy way to keep track of how much money you spent on a credit card. Pre-internet, you'd get a surprise at the end of the month when your bill came in the mail. The good news is that now we have these credit card apps where we can go in and check our balance *at any time*.

My recommendation? Check your balance once a week. Do it on Friday afternoon, when you're in a good mood.

Funny thing about pressing the credit card app button on your phone: It takes effort. Because nobody likes to get bad news. And my guess is that four times out of five, when you press the credit card app button on your phone, you will get bad news.

I have a general idea of how much I am spending on my credit cards—we all do. I keep track of the big purchases. But it's easy to forget about the little stuff—all the trips you made to Chipotle. It adds up.

Pushing the button is going to be unpleasant. So why do something that is unpleasant?

The answer is simple: so that you can make a course correction before the end of the month if necessary. If you have $3,000 in your checking account and you check your credit card balance halfway through the month, and it's $2,000, you know that you are going to have to significantly slow down your spending so that you can pay your balance in full at the end of the month. If you didn't push the button, you wouldn't have this information, and you would keep spending.

Part of this is doing the hard things, man. Some people like to call this discipline. I didn't say it would be easy.

Like I said before, 25 years ago, we didn't have the ability to check our balance mid-month. All you have to do these days is to move your thumb one freaking millimeter over the button. The easiest thing in the world, and yet so hard. I get it. But you've got to do it. I do it and so should you.

And at the end of the month, I always go back and look at my spending and think, "Did I need that? Was it worth it?" This prevents me from spending money on dumb stuff the next month. It's a process of constant improvement.

Consider your
spending habits

How do you keep a low balance in the first place? That's part of a bigger philosophy about spending; thinking about the things that you need and don't need.

Some people think that they have to buy something every time they walk into a store. I know people like this. It is possible to walk into a store and not buy something. It is possible to log into Amazon and not buy something.

Two things to ask yourself about your spending habits:

1. *How much money do you spend in a day?* I read an article about five years ago that said that the average American spends $67 a day. That will be even higher now with inflation, but you get the idea. That's $67 without any housing expenses, so exclusive of your rent or mortgage. I think about this a lot. I will get home at the end of the day and think that I spent $20 on lunch, and $50 on gas. I spent $70 that day—not a bad day of spending. But then you get the cable bill, and the HOA bill, and the exterminator bill, and it starts adding up very quickly. When you make your budget, I highly recommend you not only figure out the money you spend over the course of a month, but what that works out to on a daily basis. You will find that there is not much in the way of room for discretionary expenses.

2. *How much unnecessary stuff do you buy?* I have a great deal of stuff in my house. We've been living in the same house for seven years, and when we moved in, the house was empty. It was bigger than what we were used to, and now it is full of stuff. I have no desire to put anything else in

my house. I'm 49 years old and I have twenty-six years' worth of stuff. I'm not suggesting you pursue a course of financial minimalism, and live out of a van, though some people do this. I don't feel trapped by my possessions. But if I am on vacation in Cancun, I am not going to buy a souvenir coffee mug to put with the rest of my 30 coffee mugs. After a while, you have a sense of which possessions are meaningful and which are not.

Don't get card crazy

A lot of people put a lot of brainpower into how many cards they should have. You can google it, or better yet, I'll tell you— the typical answer is four or five. I suggest three.

You need more than one—there will be situations when your credit card gets declined and you need a backup. And you probably need a backup for the backup. I have four, because I opened a fourth card to save $1,000 when I went on a mega-clothes shopping run in New York in 2012. The $1,000 off my purchase was an incentive to open up a store-brand credit card. By the way, don't do this.

Think about how stressful it would be to be juggling due dates and balances on five or more credit cards. The less complexity, the better.

One answer, I suppose, is debit cards. You should have one debit card on hand along with your three credit cards. But the same problems exist with debit cards—it's hard to keep track of how much you're spending. Then you're in overdraft hell, getting charged $20 a pop. Banks make billions of dollars a year off overdraft fees, which is the best stupid tax known to mankind.

I don't use debit cards personally. I put everything on the

credit card and pay it off at the end of the month. That way I get the points.

A few points on points

People have an unhealthy obsession with points. Which is bizarre, because the vast majority of points and miles go unused and expire worthless. People spend all this time focusing on which cards get them the most points and miles, and then never cash them in.

The credit card companies are very shrewd—notice that they market cards on the basis of *points* and *rewards*. Cards aren't marketed based on which ones have the lowest interest rates. Right? Have you ever, ever seen a credit card commercial that advertises lower interest rates? The points are free marketing for the credit card companies because it costs them virtually nothing. Everyone gets excited about the points, and then never uses them.

I accumulate a fair amount of points and miles, and I use them. I get free flights about once or twice a year. Every once in a great while I will use points to get a hotel room in Vegas. **But the thing to remember about points and miles is that you end up spending more money in the long run.** If you use miles to fly somewhere, you will have to spend money on a rental car, hotel room, and food. It's not an effective tool to limit consumption. Yes, you're getting something for free, but you're taking a costly trip that you wouldn't have otherwise taken.

Also, people aren't very good at doing the math on points. It's not a lot of money. Generally, you are saving 1–2% of your purchases. This means that if you are spending $10,000 a year on your card, you are getting only $100 back. If you have a card that saves you 5% on gas, remember that the typical person spends about $3,000 in gas a year, so it's only $150. Meanwhile, these same people will be carrying huge balances and accruing thousands of dollars in interest charges.

Which brings me to my final point on points: if you are carrying a balance of any size on your card, then it makes no sense to focus on points. You are spending more on interest than you are saving on points. *Points are only for people who pay off their balance every month.*

I should take a second here to talk about cash-back cards, like Discover, where you can get money to apply against your statement balance instead of getting points. From a personal finance standpoint, cash-back cards are generally better, because when you use points, you end up spending even more money. I know, I know, cash-back cards are boring. That's the whole idea.

Should you stress about high interest rates?

Why are interest rates so high on credit cards? Are they loan sharks?

Not really. First of all, the overhead on a credit card company is massive. They have a lot of technology, a lot of call centers, they manufacture those plastic cards, and they do lots of advertising. Then in 2009 the government passed legislation that forbade the credit card companies from raising interest rates. Now, they just start everyone at a much higher rate, which is close to 20%. Before this legislation, credit card interest rates were around 12–14%. I would not characterize this as progress.

A credit card company is a bank, and when you get a card, you open a bank account. Although it's kind of like a backwards bank account—instead of depositing money and earning interest, you are withdrawing money and paying interest. Banks make money by borrowing at a lower interest rate and lending (to you) at a higher interest rate. They earn the spread in between, after covering their expenses. Credit card lending is not what I would call an amazingly profitable business. It's very cyclical. Once in a while, a recession comes along, and people lose their jobs, and default on their credit card loans. The card companies got monkeyhammered during the 2007–08 financial crisis. I'm not asking you to feel sorry for the credit card companies, but know that it's a risky business.

Credit card loans are risky loans because they are *unsecured*. They are not secured by real property. Mortgages aren't all that risky because if you stop paying the mortgage, the bank can foreclose and take the house. Same with car loans. If you stop making the payments, here comes the repo man. They can sell the car and recoup most of the money.

But credit card borrowing isn't secured by anything. There is nothing for the lender to repossess. If they want their money, all they can do is to beg and plead—they can call you at all hours of the day and harass you. But if you stop paying on an $80,000 balance, there is not much the credit card company can do. That is the main reason that interest rates on credit cards are higher than anything else—in case you were wondering why you pay 20% interest on a credit card. There is a real reason for it. The bank has to compensate for the increased risk.

There was only one time in my life when I didn't pay off my entire credit card balance. I wanted to see what would happen if I didn't. I got charged $50 in interest, that's what happened. Every other time I have paid the entire balance. Every time, including when I made big purchases. As I said before, when

I make a big purchase on a credit card, I make sure it is cash-secured. I absolutely must have the cash in the bank account to cover the purchase; otherwise I don't do it.

At the moment, interest rates on credit cards are about 19%. If you carry a $10,000 balance on your credit card over the course of a year, you will pay $1,900 in interest. You will actually pay more than that, due to *compounding*. Is paying that interest fun? Do you get anything out of it?

If the goal is to borrow money, go to the bank and get a personal loan at 8%. It will feel very much like a loan. There will be a guy in a teal shirt and a black tie who will sit down with you in an office and sign some paperwork, and then you will make payments every month until it is paid off. That's what a loan feels like.

Should you stress about credit scores?

The credit card companies calculate the risk of individual borrowers through credit scores. The scores range from 300 to 850, where 300 is a dipstick and 850 is Richie Rich. Although the scores are not super correlated with income—it's all about your habits around borrowing.

I have not met anyone with a score less than 500, though I suppose they exist. I had an 850 score for a while, but then I paid off my mortgage, and my score went *down* (which we will discuss shortly).

People generally know what their credit score is and what makes it go up and down. It used to be that getting your credit score was an expensive hassle, but now there are a bunch of apps and credit card companies that provide it for free. **The two things that make it go up and down are paying your bills on time, and your debt utilization ratio.**

I would not get too concerned about credit scores. The average score has gone up by a lot. Americans have gotten a lot smarter about their credit in recent years.

The interesting thing about credit scores is that lenders use them as a mathematical measure of *character*. But a specific type of character: your behavior around borrowing money. Paying your bills on time is pretty straightforward. Don't be a slob, be proactive. Set a reminder on your phone to pay your bill every month. Set multiple reminders if necessary. One missed payment can reduce your score by a full 70–100 points.

Implicitly, credit scores measure your conscientiousness and organizational skills. If you're organized and pay on time, you'll have a high score. If you forget and you're late, you'll have a low score. And if you have a low score, you'll get higher interest rates when you apply for loans, or you will be turned down for loans. Imagine finding the house of your dreams and not being able to qualify for a mortgage.

The customer should always be bad

Debt utilization measures how much available credit you're using. If you have a credit card with a $20,000 limit and you have a $10,000 balance, you have a 50% debt utilization. You're using half your available credit. Credit card companies like to see this ratio below 20–30%. If you're using nearly all your available credit, then credit card companies will have a skeptical view of your finances. It means that you might one day apply for additional credit, and the credit card companies won't approve it.

High debt utilization has the potential to lower your credit score a lot. I know people that have made every single payment—every single one—and yet have a credit score in the 600s, in subprime territory. These are the customers that credit card companies want. The people who have huge balances and pay massive amounts of interest. They are good customers of the bank. They are making the bank richer and, in the process, they are getting poorer and poorer.

For what it's worth, you want to be a *bad* customer of the bank. You want to be an unprofitable customer. Do this by paying off your balance every month, and cashing in all your points. The bank will still make a little money off you, mainly through fees (such as annual fees, usage fees, balance transfer fees, and late fees), but not as much as the person who is carrying $80,000 in balances.

I don't want you to get the impression that I am anti-bank. Years after the Great Financial Crisis, people still have a pretty dim view of banks and bankers. But a lot of nice people work at banks. Generally, bankers are friendly and helpful; they want to assist you in achieving your financial goals. How would you buy a house without a bank? And the rates that they charge these days are certainly not usurious. The banks don't determine interest rates—a bank CEO doesn't "decide" the interest rate you are going to pay on your mortgage. This is determined by market forces.

Ironically, credit card companies are very *nice*. If you run into trouble, you can call them up and they will help put you on a payment plan that works for you, without all the interest and penalties. This is for real. Try it sometime. Call up your credit card company and navigate the stupid menu.

Once you get a real person on the phone, tell them that you're having financial difficulties and ask if there's anything they can do. A good acting job might help. Their response will shock you. They'll bend over backwards to help you. If you go bankrupt, they will get none of their money back. If they know there's a risk of that, they will try to get some or most of their money back, by proposing a solution that works for everyone. Such is the nature of unsecured lending. People are basically on the honor system.

And if you run out of options...

We should take this opportunity to talk about bankruptcy, which should be a last resort. But in many cases, it's not the worst option.

The worst option is limping along for years, unable to get out from a giant load of debt, with all your free cash flow going to interest on credit card balances. Debt can be crippling. If you're at the point of no return, declaring bankruptcy might not be a bad idea.

There are consequences to this, including consequences that you might not have even thought of. If you've ever declared bankruptcy, that will prevent you from ever working in the financial industry. It stays on your credit report for a period of ten years, and your credit score will go down the toilet. You won't be borrowing any money for a while. You'll be using things like secured credit cards (prepaid credit cards, in other words) to get your score back up. It's no fun. I don't want to make it seem like it's the answer to all your problems, but it might be better than the alternative.

Honestly, if it were possible to go back to the days before credit cards, I would. Think about this. Studies show that the existence of credit cards increases consumption by 10%. That means we are buying 10% more stuff than we would if we only had cash. And all that stuff creates interest for the credit card companies, *which wouldn't exist if we didn't carry balances*. That's right. If everyone paid their bill in full every month, credit card companies would shrivel up and blow away. Or at least, their stocks would go down 80%.

Again, I like banks, and people who work at banks are nice people, but there is a parasitic aspect to this that I just can't get past. The only discernible benefit to credit cards is that we get to have our $500 jacket three months sooner. I guess that is something. But in the absence of credit cards, we would have delayed gratification—people would save for three months and then buy the jacket, which is how it should be.

I disapprove of all of this. But it's the American way. We love debt.

I don't love debt, because debt is the chief activator of our financial stress. People really do go bankrupt, you know. Hundreds of thousands of people a year. And that is in the good years. That is a lot of stress and a lot of misery that is inflicted by credit cards. And it is all unnecessary.

....

I have never, ever experienced any financial stress relating to credit cards. Which makes sense because I only ever carried a balance that one time. Then again, I am not a big spender, and even at my current high level of income, I save up for stuff. I set financial goals. If there is something fancy that I want to buy, I set a goal that I will make x amount of money before I buy it. I don't put it on the credit card and worry about paying for it later. That is not a habit of highly effective people. Never YOLO. You need to take this seriously.

I do want to tell you one quick story about how I ran into trouble with a credit card company—and how it could happen to anyone.

In 2000, I had a branded Coast Guard Academy Alumni Association credit card from MBNA. You might recall that Bank of America acquired MBNA a few years later. It was one of three credit cards I had. I was in grad school at the time, and a big-time CF. I couldn't afford to be anything else, so I wasn't putting much on the card. $50 one month, $100 the next month. Keep in mind that this was before credit card payments went online. I was still getting paper statements.

This was the time that I got the job offer from Lehman Brothers in New York City, and we were going to be moving back to the East Coast. We had connected with a real estate agent in New Jersey, who was helping us shop for condos. The real estate agent hooked me up with a mortgage lender, who was going to preapprove me for a mortgage. I wasn't worried at all—like I said, I always make my payments on time.

One day I got a call from the mortgage lender. They told me they couldn't preapprove me for a loan, because my credit score was too low and one of my credit card accounts was in collection.

What?

I asked them which account, and they said it was my MBNA account. I called up MBNA to find out what was going on. It occurred to me that I hadn't received a statement from MBNA in months. They were either all getting lost in the mail (unlikely) or they stopped sending them to me.

The MBNA representative was not cool. Not cool at all. I told him that they stopped sending me statements, and this guy told me, "Mr. Dillian, it is your responsibility to pay what you owe whether we send you a statement or not." I had a $54 charge on the account that turned into $600 over a period of months after interest, penalties, and fees. I offered to pay the

$600 on the spot. I settled the matter by paying the balance and closing the account. The representative said that he would restore my credit score to its original state, which he did. I ended up getting the mortgage.

I still wonder about that situation to this day. Think about it—you're MBNA, and you have this unprofitable customer, a CF who charges $50 a month. Why not stop sending him statements, hope he forgets, and rack up a bunch of fees? It is not wholly implausible. And that guy that I was on the phone with—he was right, you know. It was my responsibility to pay regardless of whether they sent me a statement or not. If I didn't get a statement, it was my responsibility to find out what the hell was going on. I just spaced. And I almost got in big trouble.

I doubt the credit card companies would try anything like that these days. Too much scrutiny, and there's places for people to complain on the internet. People would figure out pretty quickly if they were up to no good. But keep in mind that this is serious business, and these are giant faceless corporations which are not looking out for your best interests. *You have to pay attention.* This is why you must check your balance at the end of every week. If you didn't budget for that unexpected $600 hit, then you're going to feel mighty stressed.

You would get better treatment if you had a premium or VIP card, like the Amex platinum card. But 27-year-old me with a couple of thousand bucks in the bank was just a number to MBNA. There is no other explanation for it.

So mind your Ps and Qs. Credit cards can make your life easier, and better. But they can also make it infinitely worse. And remember: Never, ever be a good customer of the bank.

Next we will be talking about the largest debt you will ever have in your entire life—a mortgage on your house. Don't screw it up.

....

CHAPTER 9

Buying a House
Is Stressful

As we said before, who to marry is the most important financial decision you will make in your life.

But outside of that...

Buying a house is the second most important financial decision you will make in your life. And people routinely mess it up.

Why do they mess it up? Because buying a house is the most *emotional* financial decision you will make in your life. People lose their minds.

Let's back up a second. How do you buy a house?

How do you
buy a house?

A lot of people kick tires on houses by driving around a neighborhood they might like to live in. They come across one that has a "for sale" sign out in front of it. They take down the number of the realtor, call the realtor, and set up an appointment.

Now, the first thing the realtor is going to do is get you *prequalified* for the mortgage. This is a pretty simple process—you go to a bank, you give them your name, date of birth, social security number, and income, and they tell you if you are preapproved, and crucially, the maximum loan you can handle. The bank figures this out so that the mortgage payment, insurance, and property taxes will equal about 42% of your income, although it varies from place to place. Then you go look for the most expensive possible house you can buy.

This is bad.

The reason this is bad is because *you should not be spending more than 25% of your income on housing*. Why? Because if you do, you will be unable to pursue other financial goals, like saving for retirement. The mortgage will suck up all the available cash flow. I'm not saying you will default on the mortgage and lose the house—outside of 2008, that is actually not a very common occurrence. What I'm saying is that all your money is going to be going toward the house—and nothing else.

I will concede that in certain parts of the country, like California, it is next to impossible to spend less than 25% of your income on housing. It is simply too expensive. You have to try. You also have the option of not living in California. This is one of those *big decisions* you have to get right. If you get the house wrong, it doesn't matter how much coffee you give up— you will still be hosed.

The big thing
people get wrong

The main way to get it wrong is to get too big of a house; bigger than what you need. You actually don't need that big of a house. If you get a house that is 500 square feet smaller, you're not going to be living in that house all miserable because it's too small. You will be fine. I've lived in some small houses, and I've never been like, "This house sucks, I can't wait to get a bigger one."

People can easily forgo large luxuries, but not small luxuries.

Maintaining daily austerity on small things like coffee, food, and clothes is much more difficult to sustain. And think of it this way—if you get a smaller house, you won't have to cut corners on everything else. You will be happier, and that is what this program is all about—being happier.

For most people, buying a house is an emotional decision, not a rational decision. They go house shopping, and they find *the* house. It's perfect. They can picture living there: the kids can play in the backyard, it's walking distance to the store, it's in a great neighborhood with great schools, the couch is going to go here, the TV is going to go here, they can imagine themselves in that house, and they *have to have it.*

"Sure, it costs $100,000 more, but we qualified for that amount, so we must be able to do it." The problem is that if you buy a house that costs $100,000 more, you will pay $110,000 *more* in interest over the life of the loan, at current interest rates, assuming you don't make any prepayments. And most of that interest will be front-loaded.

I see it over and over again. This is how people get to age 45 and don't have any retirement savings.

I will say one thing: we have a peculiar system in the United States where the quality of a child's education is determined by playing the geographic lottery. You live in a good neighborhood and you go to a good school, or else you might go to a bad school. The housing values in "good" school districts tend to be inflated—because everyone wants to live there. For a lot of people, this is an overriding concern, which leads to them getting a more expensive house.

There are no solutions here, only trade-offs, as Thomas Sowell once said. Just know that it is an economic trade-off and there is a cost to getting your kid into a good school. If you're doing it, do it with your eyes open.

But yeah, buying a house is the biggest financial decision that you will make in your life; and if your hands aren't shaking when you're signing the loan documents at the closing, you do not have an appreciation of the risk involved. After all, it's hundreds of thousands (or millions) of dollars. And that is with the U.S. having a very liquid, robust, institutionalized, mainstreamed housing market—the process is actually very easy, and there are people to help you along the way. Let me tell you something— the first house that I bought, right after I turned 25, I had no idea what I was doing. I didn't know what a mortgage was or how it worked. They told me to sign here, and I signed there. I was a kid. I didn't know enough to be scared.

I have bought and sold five houses in my lifetime, and I am in the process of building a sixth. That will probably be the last one. These days, I am very comfortable with the risk—I have lots of experience doing this. Not all of the houses have been good financial decisions. And not all of the houses have been good lifestyle decisions. I've had good ones and bad ones. But I've never, ever bought more house than I can afford.

A house is
not an investment

Let's get this one out of the way—*a house is not an investment.*

Stocks are an investment. Bonds are an investment. Houses are not. Stocks and bonds pay dividends and interest. Not only does your house not pay dividends and interest, it actually *costs money to own.* You have to pay the insurance, property taxes, and utilities. And crucially, you have to pay for maintenance. A good estimate is that you will be paying 1% of the value of the house each year in maintenance, *on average.* Some years you will pay less. Other years you will have to replace the roof. But if you have a $500,000 house, you are going to pay $5,000 a year in maintenance, on average.

You don't have to pay taxes and insurance and maintenance on your stocks. So we say that stocks and bonds are positive carry, and a house is negative carry. Furthermore, a house will physically depreciate over time. Just like your car, but a bit more slowly. If you were to live in a house for 50 years, at the end of 50 years, it could be a worse house in a worse neighborhood. That's how it goes.

But people say, "Housing prices go up over time!"
Do they?

For a period of time in the late 2000s, they didn't, and there's no rule that says that housing prices must go up over time. They might go down. At the time of writing, housing prices have gone up a lot due to a number of macro factors, and one of them is underbuilding—we simply didn't build enough houses post-financial crisis to keep up with population growth. Another is interest rates, which went down a lot. But the conditions that led to today's housing prices might one day change, and lead to lower housing prices. It's an asset—it can go up or down. And we found out what happened during the financial crisis when houses go down.

Having said all that, yes, it is true that housing prices go up over time (about 4% annually, in fact, keeping up with inflation); and yes, it is true that sometimes they go up a lot. It is also true that many people invest in real estate and do as well or better than if they had invested in stocks. Real estate investment takes very specialized knowledge that is very different from security valuation. Let's just say that for personal finance purposes, a house is not an investment; but for investment purposes, it could be. In reality, it is both. It is something you live in and consume that also generally increases in value over time, subject to where you live in the world and other factors.

Some people pay cash for a house, but most of us don't. We place a 20% down payment, and borrow the rest. This is the reason that buying a house is the riskiest decision you will ever make—because of the leverage involved.

Let's say you buy a $500,000 house, which is a little more expensive than the typical home. You put down a $100,000 down payment, or 20%. If the price of the house goes from $500,000 to $600,000, the equity in your house will go from $100,000 to $200,000. You had a 100% return on your money, even though you only put 20% down.

Now, if the value of the house declines to $400,000, then your equity is wiped out, and you have a negative 100% return on your money. You lost everything. And if the price of the house goes down more than that, you are *underwater* on the house, which means that if you sold it, you would have to pay to get out. This is the position that so many people found themselves in in 2008; underwater on their houses, and trapped. Your hands should be shaking when you sign the loan documents.

I'm not saying it will happen again… but I'm saying it *could* happen again. There is risk in everything you do. Fifteen years later and people already have complete amnesia about what happened in 2008. Housing prices don't always go up. You need to have a contingency plan for if they don't.

Mortgages

Let's talk about what a mortgage is. A mortgage is a loan, secured by real property. Most of the time, mortgages are not risky loans for the banks to make. If you don't pay the mortgage, they kick you out of the house and sell it, and get most of their money back. This is why interest rates on mortgages are so low compared to interest rates on credit cards and other loans.

The other reason why interest rates are so low is because of the government-sponsored enterprises (GSEs), like Fannie Mae and Freddie Mac. You may have heard of these guys before. What do they do?

Well, interestingly enough, in the U.S. we have a very capitalist country with a very socialized residential real estate market. Fannie and Freddie securitize mortgages. What that means is that they buy individual mortgages from banks, put them in a pool, the pool of mortgages pays out the interest and principal payments from all the mortgages in the pool, and then sells them as bonds known as mortgage-backed securities (MBS). Investors from all over the world buy these mortgage-backed securities.

So when you make your mortgage payments to the bank, there is a very high likelihood that you're not making them to the bank—you're making them to some faceless investor in Denmark or something like that. If you get the bill from the bank, it's because the bank continues to *service* the mortgage, and at some point over the life of the loan, it may be taken over by another servicer.

In the old days, a bank would hold the loan on its balance sheet, and if you didn't pay the loan, you would be hurting the bank. Now, you're hurting the anonymous guy in Denmark. Mortgage securitization is a miraculous thing, and it has redefined the relationship between the borrower and the lender. Nowadays, the bank wants to get the mortgage off its balance sheet so it is free to make new loans and collect origination fees.

Then something interesting happens—Fannie and Freddie issue a bunch of debt in the capital markets, and raise money so that they can buy back the MBS they just issued. They hold thousands of MBS with millions of mortgages, collecting interest and principal. But there's a lot of risk associated with this.

First of all, this portfolio of mortgages is very sensitive to interest rates, and an adverse move up or down will hurt them. But Fannie and Freddie are also in trouble if people stop paying their mortgages, which is what happened in 2008. They lost over a hundred billion dollars, and had to be bailed out by the government. Fannie and Freddie went bankrupt, and ended up in government conservatorship, where they have been for the last 15 years. There have been some efforts to get them out of conservatorship, and restore them as private companies, but that turned into a political football and nothing is going to change anytime soon. The result is that we have a housing market that is very heavily subsidized by taxpayers.

If you're wondering how all this benefits you, there are some studies which have shown that mortgage rates would be about a percent higher if it weren't for the GSEs. So all of this saves you a couple hundred bucks a month.

But that's not all. In the U.S. we also have FHA and VA loans, for low-income borrowers and veterans, respectively. If you have an opportunity to buy a home with a VA or FHA loan, I suggest you pass.

With a VA loan, you can get 100% financing—no down payment; and with an FHA loan, you only have to put 3.5% down. You might think this is great—no down payment! It's actually the worst thing in the world. If you give someone a loan with 100% financing, you are not doing them any favors. And the reason is that it is very, very difficult to build equity on a loan with little or no down payment.

For example, if you were to get a VA loan with 100% financing, it would take you almost ten years just to get to 20% equity. This means that you're pretty much in the house forever, because even if prices don't move, you will have about 6% in transaction costs in selling the house, and if you don't have the cash, you won't be able to move. You're underwater from the beginning. It's all bad.

You may not know this about FHA and VA loans. These are securitized, too, by a different agency: Ginnie Mae. And Ginnie Mae packages up these loans into bonds and sells them just like Fannie and Freddie. But Ginnie Mae MBS are backed by the full faith and credit of the U.S. government, meaning that they are essentially insured. So if XYZ ding-dong defaults on his FHA loan, taxpayers have to foot the bill. I am not making this up. Thankfully, FHA and VA loans still represent a pretty small part over the overall mortgage market. The rest of us have to put down 20%.

And that's a good thing. Nobody is doing anybody any favors with 100% financing.

If you're getting an expensive house, then there is a pretty good chance that you will end up with a jumbo loan. Fannie Mae and Freddie Mac securitize mortgages up to a certain size (known as conforming loans), and beyond that, you'll have a jumbo mortgage. Jumbo rates are typically higher (though sometimes lower), because the market for large loans is less liquid, because of a lack of securitization. If you end up with a jumbo mortgage, don't fret, there is nothing exotic about it. It is just a mortgage that is bigger.

Occasionally these loans have a recasting feature, which means that when you submit additional principal, instead of shortening the duration of the mortgage, it actually makes the payment smaller, which is awesome. If you have the opportunity to get a loan with a recasting feature, I highly recommend it.

Loan-to-value

Even though you are required to put down a minimum of 20% on a home purchase, you should actually put down *more* if you can. You'll have a larger equity cushion, and your payments will be smaller. I put 35% down on the house that I bought in 2015, and I never regretted that for one second.

In the mortgage industry, this is known as something called "LTV," which stands for loan-to-value. LTV measures the ratio of the mortgage to the value of the house. For example: since I put down 35%, my LTV was 65%—the loan was 65% of the value of the house.

The interesting thing about LTV is that it is the *number one predictor of default*. Think about it—if you don't have any equity in the house, it's very easy to say FU, and mail your keys to the bank. You're walking away from nothing. But someone who has 35% equity is very unlikely to walk away from the mortgage, even if they can't make the payment. They'll figure something out; otherwise their equity will be stranded. During the financial crisis, housing prices went down a lot, and everyone's equity disappeared, which is why they went to youwalkaway.com—all the LTVs went to 100% or more. So it's in your best interest (and the bank's best interest) to put down as big a down payment as possible. Everybody wins.

Speaking of which, on the rare occasion that a bank allows you to put less than 20% down, you have to pay something called PMI—Private Mortgage Insurance. Basically, you have to purchase insurance on the mortgage on behalf of the lender. It's not a lot of money, but it's a nuisance. And it's not a good idea to put less money down, for the reasons I already mentioned. *Having said all that*, I only put 15% down on my first house (a condo), and everything worked out fine, to say the least. And I paid the PMI the entire time.

The 30-year mortgage

The 30-year, fixed-rate residential mortgage was probably the most important financial innovation of the 20th century. Why? Because it allowed people to build wealth in the process of paying their mortgage over time.

Think about it. There are a lot of people out there who suck at saving. They can't save a thing. But you know what they can do? They can make payments on a mortgage. And embedded in every mortgage payment is a principal payment. As people make these payments, their equity grows over time.

I live in the Myrtle Beach area. I can't tell you how many people move here from places like Brooklyn—they bought their house in the late 1970s for $70,000, paid the mortgage, sold it for $900,000, and moved down south. They bought a house for $250,000 in cash and lived off the rest—without ever saving a dollar in the bank or ever contributing to a retirement account. It was the combination of building equity over time, and a rise in housing prices over a generation, that made them fantastically wealthy—even though they were blue-collar workers. It's really powerful stuff. For a lot of people, literally all of their wealth is tied up in the house.

Now, that's not a good idea. We will talk about asset allocation in Part IV, and how much of your money should be allocated to real estate (generally around 20%), and how if all of your money is stuffed into one single asset, you certainly want some diversification—but a lot of people don't diversify, and it works out fine for them. I don't know whether home prices will go up or down in any given year, but I feel pretty comfortable predicting that they will go up over a 30-year timeframe.

The thing with the 30-year mortgage is that it really made more sense in an age when people didn't move around as much. They got a job at the factory, worked there for 30 years, and lived in the same house. Now people are more mobile (although mobility is actually declining somewhat, tragically).

I don't know too many people who live in a house for 30 years these days. So perhaps it makes sense to get a mortgage of a shorter duration? The 15-year mortgage is an excellent solution, but a lot of people don't like it because the payments are higher. This is true, but those payments will have a much higher percentage going to principal than a 30-year mortgage, and you will build equity much faster.

I have a rule about this: you can get a 30-year mortgage if you like, but make sure you can afford the house only if you qualify for a 15-year mortgage. If you're getting a 30-year mortgage because you have to, not because you want to, then you shouldn't buy the house—the house is too big and too expensive. And more importantly, it will cause you a lot of stress.

Prepaying

A 30-year fixed rate mortgage is a magical thing, because it gives you *the option to prepay*. If you've ever owned a house, and you've made a payment either online or by check, then you know that there is a box where you can write in *additional principal*—extra money that you're going to use to pay down the balance of the loan.

There are competing philosophies on this. I know some people who say that you should never prepay your mortgage because you lose liquidity—once you send in that money, you can't get it out. Wrong. You should prepay your mortgage as quickly as possible, and the goal should be to pay the whole thing off in 10 years. That may sound unrealistic, but it really isn't—my last mortgage I paid off in 3.5 years.

Why do this? Because any time you send in additional principal, you are shortening the duration of the mortgage— if you get a $300,000 mortgage and send in an extra $250/ month, now you have a 24-year mortgage instead of a 30-year mortgage, and you won't have to pay any interest in the last six years of the loan. That is big savings.

I'm sure if you took this advice and you showed it to a banker or a Wall Street person, they would be like, "That is terrible advice—if you have a 3% mortgage and you have the opportunity to invest in the stock market at 10%, you should do that. Borrow at 3% and invest at 10%."

Except the returns of the stock market vary, and are not fixed at 10%; and while you might be happy some years, other years you will not be so happy. And moreover, borrowing money to buy stocks is a dumb idea that will cause you huge amounts of stress. If you have cash hanging around, send it toward the mortgage, prepay as much as you can, and save yourself all the interest expense.

A lot of people think of this problem in terms of interest rates: borrow at 3%, invest at 10%. I think of this in terms of *dollars spent in interest*. The less you spend in interest, the more you have to contribute to your 401(k) or simply buy stuff you want. Besides, you may think that you can earn 10% in the stock market, but people suck at investing, and there is a good chance that you are going to lose money, and then you will have debt and losses (and stress).

By the way, a tiny percentage of mortgages have what's known as a prepayment penalty, which is what it sounds like— you have to pay a penalty if you prepay or refinance your mortgage. That loan document that you sign at the closing is pretty big and intimidating, but you should read it carefully to make sure that there are no prepayment penalties. Even better, just ask the banker point-blank if there is one. By the way, very large loans (in the millions) made to celebrities and super-rich people generally have prepayment penalties, because there is so much interest rate risk for the bank.

Refinancing

There is a special kind of prepayment known as *refinancing*. This is when interest rates drop, and you can refinance the loan to a new mortgage rate. Most people don't understand the mechanics behind this process—basically, you're getting a bank to issue a new loan which will pay off the old loan. If you've ever tried refinancing your mortgage, you probably wondered why a bank requires an appraisal and all kinds of bureaucratic paperwork just to drop the rate. It's because they're issuing a whole new loan, and they have to go through the origination process all over again.

Going back to the MBS that we discussed earlier, the bondholder is actually very unhappy when people refinance their mortgages, because they suddenly get a huge slug of cash (which pays off the mortgage), and since interest rates have dropped, they have to take the cash and reinvest it at a lower rate. That's why the prepayment option on mortgages is so magical—why the banks let people do this is beyond me.

Other types of mortgages

There are other types of mortgages than 30-year and 15-year fixed these days, although they are much less common. You have pure adjustable-rate mortgages (ARMs), where the interest rate adjusts up or down each year based on some benchmark. You have what's known as hybrid ARMs, where the rate is fixed for a set amount of time (typically three, five, or seven years) and then adjusts after that.

Most people are terrified of adjustable-rate mortgages, because what if the interest rate goes up? What if your mortgage payment doubles? Not unreasonable, I suppose, but it's pretty rare that mortgage rates move that fast (though that happened in 2022); and in the case of hybrid ARMs, you can take the first three/five/seven years to pay off as much of the loan balance as possible before the rate adjusts. I actually had a 5/1 ARM in the 2000s and after the five-year rate lock was finished, rates dropped and my mortgage payment become much smaller. Having said all that, and though you didn't buy this book for a macroeconomic forecast, I have a hard time seeing how interest rates are going to go much lower than they already are.

There is a good chance that going forward, you will never refinance your mortgage, and you will never get an ARM or hybrid ARM. Even if interest rates don't go up, they're unlikely to go down much more.

....

The key here is to buy a house that you can afford. Remember, it's not a million little things that determine whether you have money, it's a handful of big things: the house, the car, and the student loans. Get these three things right, and you won't have to worry about the little things. The primary way people screw this up is by getting too big of a house.

The primary way that people end up with too big of a house is because it turns into an emotional decision; they fall in love with the house. Pay no more than 25% of your income on housing-related expenses, and only get a house if you can afford it with a 15-year mortgage, whether you end up getting a 15-year mortgage or not. That's the best advice I can give.

I truly want everyone who reads this book to one day be able to live in a giant mansion—you deserve it. Everyone should one day have the experience of living in a giant house. But baby steps. You will get there over time, if you're smart.

Next we're going to talk about paying for a college education—a controversial subject these days.

....

CHAPTER 10

Going to School Is Stressful

T he state of higher education in the U.S. is really sad. You have people with hundreds of thousands of dollars in student debt, with no realistic way of paying it back. And they're mad, and looking for someone to blame.

Let's talk about it.

The big questions

During the Great Financial Crisis in 2009, we effectively eliminated private student lending. We nationalized it. All student lending is now done by the government. Which raises a lot of questions, right?

If the government is making these student loans, why do they care if they get paid back? Why are the interest rates so high? Why is it that people faithfully made their student loan payments for ten years and now the loan balance is higher than when they started? And moreover, why is going to college so expensive?

Where do we begin?

Well, for starters, the government never intended for people to go to college for free (though we might get there eventually). So, you take out a loan, and you have to pay it back. During the pandemic, borrowers were granted forbearance for a period of many months, which got people wondering if the government would *ever* require these loans to be paid back. Currently, there are $1.7 trillion in student loans outstanding. If the government wanted to forgive those loans, it would simply take them on the balance sheet, go $1.7 trillion further into debt, raise $1.7 trillion in taxes, or a combination of the two. At the time of writing, there is little appetite to go further into debt or raise taxes, so I think we are stuck with the student loans for now.

Why are the interest rates so high? Arguably, they are not high enough! Student loans are issued to unknown borrowers with unknown credit. Nobody checks your credit score when you get a student loan. If you can fog a mirror, you get money. Remember our earlier discussion about secured and unsecured debt. Student loans are unsecured debt—there is nothing to repossess. The government can make your life miserable for not paying back your loans, but they can't take your house or your car. Student loans are actually issued at a below-market interest rate, relative to the risk to the lender.

Why is your loan balance going up even though you are making payments? Thanks, Obama. In 2009, then-president

Obama signed into law something called income-based repayment plans. Upon graduation, you get a job and the government looks at your income and says, "Okay, here is the payment you can afford." But that payment is likely to be far smaller than it takes to pay off the loan over any extended period of time. If you borrowed $200,000, your payment should be around $800 a month, but instead it is $200 a month. You are shielded from the economic consequences of your decision—temporarily. The government then takes the interest that you didn't pay and adds it to the loan balance. For a period of time in the 2000s, they had something similar in the mortgage market: they were called negative amortization loans. You pay a portion of the payment, and the rest gets added to the back end. Needless to say, most of these loans failed and banks don't make negative amortization loans anymore, because they suck and they are unfair.

It's appalling that the government gets away with this. People think they are paying down their student loans, but they don't understand the math behind how the loans work, the loans get bigger over time, and then they want to vote for Bernie Sanders. I could not come up with a crueler system if I tried. If you are on one of these income-based repayment plans, my suggestion would be to pay *more money*—perhaps much more—to chip away at the loan balance.

But the biggest reason that student loans are the worst thing in the world is because *you cannot discharge them in bankruptcy*. Sure, you can declare bankruptcy, and get rid of your car loan, your credit card debt, and your mortgage—but the student loans never go away. You can never get rid of them. The only way to get rid of them is to pay them off. And some people can't. They borrowed $300,000 to go to a third-tier law school and they're making $40,000 a year as an attorney. It is checkmate.

The only way to get out of this is to *make more money*. It

doesn't matter that you went to school to be a lawyer—you will have to do something else. This is too bad. People get suicidal over student loans. They are trapped.

The craziest story I ever heard: a friend of mine did some charity work with the homeless in New York City. Frequently they were drug addicts. He worked with a guy that had been homeless for 17 years, and was addicted to drugs. The guy got sober, cleaned himself up, and got his first job in 17 years, working at McDonald's. Within *days*, a couple of guys showed up at McDonald's looking for money for his student loans. When he got the job, his social security number hit the system and he popped back up on the grid. Seventeen years later, the government still wanted its money. And it was going to garnish a portion of his $10 an hour wages.

Dude, this is really bad. Take student loans seriously. You cannot get rid of this debt—ever. I mean, the fairest thing we could do is to make the loans dischargeable in bankruptcy, but if people can default on their student loans, then you have to start doing credit checks, or raising interest rates—a lot—or a combination of the two. Which would probably be a good thing. This would have the effect of people borrowing less money, and going to cheaper schools, or not going to school at all, which would drive the cost down.

Which gets us to: why is going to college so expensive? Because by lending an unlimited amount of money at low interest rates, the government is implicitly subsidizing higher education. Colleges and universities can charge whatever they want, because people have unlimited money (which they borrowed) to pay for it. If Harvard cost $200,000 a year, people would be able to borrow that money. Colleges and universities have been taking that money and spending it in a variety of ways, on better athletic facilities, the Starbucks climbing wall, and lots and lots of administration.

Interestingly enough, that money has not gone to faculty—professors are as underpaid as ever. But frequently a university will have dozens or even hundreds of assistant deans and vice associate provosts making multiple six figures. Layers upon layers of management. It wouldn't be hard to cut costs in higher education, but there is absolutely no incentive to do so, as long as the money keeps coming in.

In recent years, we've heard a number of conservative pundits talk about the fact that perhaps not so many people should be going to college—they should be learning a trade, instead. Kaylee with her $100,000 psychology degree is going to end up waiting tables, whereas a higher-paying career might have been available to her if she went to tech school and learned how to turn a wrench. That ignites a debate about why people go to college in the first place—is it to be well-rounded, educated citizens, or is it solely to get a high-paying job? Hopefully a balance of the two. But there are some degrees—like film studies, for example—which make you not-well qualified to do anything in particular after graduation. If you're spending six figures on a degree, and it doesn't get you a job, that education you received is a luxury, and you better have the money to pay for it.

The problem with people graduating from college with too much debt (aside from the obvious) is that debt makes it impossible to get married, buy a house, have kids, or do anything you want to do in life. An economist would say that it hinders household formation. So all you have is debt and rent. The millennials are just getting around to buying houses, after a long delay, now that they are approaching their 40s. Up until this point, they weren't able to do so.

I was one of the lucky ones. I went to a U.S. service academy (partly to avoid student loans), and went to school for free. Not exactly free—I had a five-year service commitment afterwards, which included a lot of puking off the side of a boat in the Pacific Northwest. Definitely not the easiest way to get a free education. But graduating without student loans was a very big deal, and put me far ahead of my peer group in terms of financial development.

I later went to business school while I was working, paid for most of it as I went, and ended up with $15,000 in student loans. I made payments on the student loans for six months, then once I got my first bonus I promptly paid them off. Of course, school was a lot cheaper back then—my entire MBA (at an expensive private school) cost $45,000. I know, I know, I'm a lucky Generation Xer.

Grad school is actually where most of the problem lies. It's supply and demand—we're simply making too many PhD programs for the jobs available. PhD (or masters) programs are very profitable for universities, so new graduate programs open across the country every year. You may think that if you get a PhD you will be able to teach at a university, but it is *highly* competitive—there are hundreds of applicants for every position, and typically only people from the top three to five schools get those tenure-track jobs. Everyone else is an adjunct, making $3,000 a course. These are some very disillusioned people. The advice I've heard on grad school is that you shouldn't go unless someone else is paying.

I went to grad school a second time, very recently, to get my MFA in Writing—a dream that I've had since I was 22 years old. I don't need an MFA—when I started, I was already a two-time published author, columnist, and newsletter writer—but I wanted one anyway, and I paid out of pocket. I learned an incredible amount in my MFA program, and I'm glad I did it. It cost me around $70,000, which I could easily afford, but not everyone can. There are a lot of people who get MFAs who never do anything in particular with them.

I'm not quite sure what it is, but somehow, when it comes to higher education, all reason and accountability goes out the window and innumeracy takes over. $70,000 is a lot of money, and I imagine that most people won't spend $70,000 on a car, but they will spend it on a degree.

Perhaps it's because people view it as an investment; they can get a better job and make more money. But most of the time, that isn't true. Perhaps it's because people don't bear the true cost of the degree until much later—if you're paying $200 a month, why not? But ten years later you have $100,000 in debt instead of $70,000, and reality sets in. Perhaps it's because people get romantic about learning, and who doesn't? My three graduation days were the happiest days of my life—particularly for my MFA. Finishing an undergraduate or graduate degree is an incredible achievement.

So maybe people do it for the psychic rewards, not the financial rewards. That would seem to be the case.

How much you should pay for college

I have a system for figuring out how much you should pay for college:

Let's say you get into a top-tier school—particularly Harvard or Stanford, but any Ivy League or similar school will do. How much should you pay to go to these schools?

Anything. Whatever it costs. If it costs $300,000, you should pay it. The top schools frequently have generous scholarships for low or middle-income students, but even if you don't get one of those scholarships, you should go. There are two reasons.

First, *name brand* counts when it comes to college. A lot of times you'll have a smart kid and the parents will say, "Well, just go to the honors program at UConn, it's cheaper." The problem is that the honors programs at UConn and the top-tier schools are not the same. If there's an employer who sees a UConn résumé come across his desk, he's pitching it in the trash can. Even if the honors program is just as rigorous or more rigorous than an Ivy League school. It's about name brand; and it's also about the prestige associated with being accepted by a highly selective school. As a corollary, you don't even really have to go to Harvard for more than a year. You just have to get in.

The second reason is because of networking effects. You go to Harvard, and you are going to be there with the smartest kids in the country. A lot of those kids are going to go on to do some pretty incredible things—like starting Facebook, or running for office, or anything else. If you go to Harvard (or similar schools), you will make connections with some very wealthy, powerful people that can last a lifetime. And they will help you out. Or maybe you become one of those wealthy, powerful people. The unemployment rate coming out of Harvard is essentially zero. And nearly all of them will become millionaires or people at the top of their field—no matter what they major in.

So if you get into one of the top schools, just go, it doesn't matter how much it costs, because you will earn enough money to be able to pay off the debt within a relatively short period of time.

What if you get into a second-tier school? Here I am talking about small private liberal arts colleges, like perhaps Franklin & Marshall in Lancaster, Pennsylvania, or some of the better state schools that have a good academic reputation. Michigan comes to mind. I would suggest you can only attend these schools if you accumulate no more than $40,000 in debt—$10,000 a year.

Why? Because you simply won't have the earnings power coming out of these schools to service the debt. You will have some earnings power, but not enough to pay six figures for your education.

You should strive to pay off your student loans in five years or less.

If you can't pay off your student loans in five years, then you paid too much for your education. Someone coming out of one of these schools could conceivably earn $60,000–$70,000 a year, and paying $8,000 in student loans comes out to about 12–15% of their income, which is doable. You don't want to be one of these people who is rolling around with student loans in their 40s. Or 50s. I have heard some stories.

And finally, if you plan on attending a third-tier school, which is everything else, then you can only go if you can do it without debt. It doesn't have to be free; it just means it has to be cheap enough to pay as you go. On graduation, your earnings power will be severely limited and you won't have the ability to service any debt at all. This is where people tomahawk themselves the most—they go to a third-tier liberal arts school, pay $80,000 a year in tuition, and end up waiting tables. It happens over and over again.

Even worse than that is law school. Quick factoid: one out of every 250 people in the United States is a lawyer. In the rest of the world, it is one out of 600. When I was a kid, back in the 80s, becoming a lawyer was the ticket to wealth and success. Now, there are so many lawyers that it has driven wages down to poverty levels. I know lawyers on food stamps—I am not making this up. There are simply too many of them.

So again, if you get into Harvard Law School, go—you are going to become a senator, Supreme Court justice, or even president. If you get into a top ten law school, go. You will make lots of money in the private sector. If you get into a second-tier law school, you should probably not bother, and if you get into a third-tier law school, definitely think again. You'll spend well over $200,000 on your education and you'll come out making $40,000 a year. Don't believe me? Let your fingers do the walking, and Google some of this stuff. When people say the world doesn't need any more lawyers, it's true, but not in the way that you think. We simply have too many of them.

Medical school is a different story altogether—here people are taking on even more debt, but unless they open a family practice, they usually have the resources to pay it off. Doctors and dentists still get rich in the U.S., but that is becoming less common, as medical practices are being acquired by big hospital systems, and dental practices are being bought by private equity firms. You can still be a doctor or dentist, but you'll be an employee, rather than a proprietor—and that's a big financial difference.

Should higher education be free?

I'm sure some people are thinking it, so I will address the question: should we make higher education free?

That has been done in a few places in the world, and it hasn't worked out as expected. Argentina made college free a while back, and as a result, everyone went to college. But not everyone was serious about going to college—it attracted a lot of people who wanted to kill four years and goof around. The classroom environment deteriorated, the education deteriorated, and the universities became a shadow of what they once were—and nobody really learned anything.

In case you hadn't figured it out by now, I am of the opinion that not everyone needs to go to college—and arguably, we have too many people going as it is. The world needs ditch diggers, too, Danny. That's a not-so-nice way of saying that even in today's information age, we still need to fill a lot of jobs where people are doing physical labor with physical things. And there are big opportunities in those types of careers. The high-school graduate who started the HVAC company is probably doing $2 million a year in sales, and will one day sell that business for $10 million. Not bad for a high-school graduate. There is a roofing company in my town that is so large, I estimate that it does $50–$100 million in sales. It is a huge operation. Roofing. It would be nice if everyone could learn art history and we could raise the taste of the masses, but it costs too much.

I am a highly educated person. I have a bachelor's degree in mathematics, an MBA, and an MFA. My wife has a PhD. Most of the people I pal around with have graduate degrees. I know the value of an education. I am pretty good when I play along with *Jeopardy* at home. I know things. It's nice. And I was lucky enough to get two-thirds of this education relatively cheaply; and the last third, I paid through the nose and it didn't matter because I already had money.

The economics have changed in the last 20 years, and not for the better. You heard my solution to the problem—do credit checks on the loans—but nobody wants to do that. Nobody wants to be denied access to college because their credit score is too low. These are our options. We won't have a financial crisis because of student loans, but the debt will be subsumed onto the government balance sheet, and some of us will have to pay higher taxes.

My college experience

Speaking from personal experience, I didn't get the most out of college. I think this is typical of a lot of college students. I certainly wasn't interested in learning, outside of a couple of writing classes that I took. I enjoyed math, but the further along I went, I found it to be less useful. I had the third-highest SAT scores in my class and finished about 40% of the way down. I slept through my classes and skated by on raw intelligence.

I paid a price for this later in life, because I simply did not *learn* enough when I was in school. There are gaps in my knowledge—things that I should know and don't. Anyway, the point is that if your child goes to college, there is a 90% chance that money is going to be wasted, because 19-year-olds are partying all the time and screwing off. Those are your future business leaders, by the way. You've heard the saying: A students work for C students. B students work for the government. I'm sure there will be some point when your child is in college and you glimpse another abysmal report card. "What the hell am I doing?" you say. I totally get it.

Grad school, on the other hand, was a different story. I was super interested in learning about finance, and I got straight As in my MBA program. I was super interested in learning about writing, so I got straight As in my MFA program. You get a little maturity, you figure out what you want out of life, and you make the most of your course of study. I've had to explain numerous times to universities and employers that my undergraduate GPA (just above a 3.0) does not represent my actual potential. If I could do one thing differently in life, I would go back to college, mind my own business, and study. It is one of my greatest regrets.

....

Remember, your financial fitness is not the product of a million little things; it's a product of three big things: the house, the car, and the student loans. And if you get those big things right, you won't have to worry about the little things. And you will have a lot less stress.

I know countless people that are *really* stressed out about their student loans. They don't see a way to pay them back. And in their current occupation, they won't. They expect to die with this debt, and they probably will. That bums me out. It's sad.

I am in a big hurry to pay off debt, because of the feeling of *freedom* that you get to experience when you do. Imagine never being able to experience that freedom. Imagine some giant student loan sucking up all the available cash flow out of your budget, and never being able to enjoy some of the nicer things in life: bigger house, nicer car, clothes, food, whatever. Your financial life is full of worry—worrying about the bills, worrying about making ends meet. And it's all because of the student loans, which you can't realistically pay off.

But you can. Think back to Chapter 3: the revenue side, not the expense side. Instead of slicing and dicing the pie into smaller and smaller pieces, why not make the pie bigger? Crazy concept, except if you spent $300,000 learning to be a lawyer, then you want to be a lawyer, right? Not necessarily. You have a graduate degree. You're smart. You can do just about anything. Yes, you had your heart set on being a lawyer, but it's not working out, so... why not stop doing something that is not working?

You may have very specific training, but there's all kinds of different things you can do, if you put your mind to it. If you have a law degree or a PhD, and you're making $60,000 a year, you can increase your salary to $200,000 without a lot of effort. Student loan problem solved. But believe me when I tell you that is the *only* way out. You're not going to get there by cutting expenses. You're already eating ramen. There is no amount of expenses you can cut that is going to solve the equation. You simply have to *make more money*.

I get it. It's scary. A lot of people lack self-esteem, and they don't believe they are worth $200,000. Anything is possible. Sometime along the way, we stopped believing in our boundless potential. We believed that we could do no better. There is a 99% chance that you are not realizing your potential. *I* am not realizing my potential. But I work on it every single day. And so can you.

Next, we're going to talk about one of the most hilariously awful experiences in life—buying a car—and how to pay for it.

CHAPTER 11

....

Buying a Car
Is Stressful

S tory time.

I have never been a car guy. Why? Because a car is a stupid thing to spend money on; it depreciates, and it's money down the drain.

Up until age 47, I spent as little money on cars as possible. I have owned Toyotas my entire life because they are reliable and never break down. You can put 200,000 miles on one without breaking a sweat. I run each Toyota into the ground, then I get a new one. Rinse and repeat.

But I'm sure there's been a time when you were driving down the road and you saw a Lamborghini or a Bentley, or even something as pedestrian as a Mercedes or a BMW, and you thought to yourself, "Dang, I wish I had *that* car." You experience *envy*, and out of all material possessions, envy is strongest when it comes to cars. Because cars are a status symbol. I fell victim to this phenomenon in the spring of 2020, right before the pandemic. We are all susceptible to shiny new toys.

I was browsing online and ran across pictures of the new 2020 Corvette. The mid-engine model. The thing looked like a freaking Ferrari. I had never owned a Ferrari, or any fancy car for that matter. I had never owned a car that was a *status symbol*. Trust me, at no point in my life had someone come over to me in a parking lot and said, "Nice car." And I was way past the point where I was financially successful enough to own a nice car. Here was my thought process: I could get a Ferrari for $500,000 or a Corvette for $80,000. Seemed like a pretty good deal.

So I drove my Toyota down the road to the Chevrolet dealership, got hooked up with a salesman, and told him that I wanted to order one of the new 2020 models. The salesman had a thick Boston accent and was probably on the verge of retirement. He had a series of photos on his desk of him hanging around at racetracks with professional drivers.

I wanted a blue Corvette, one with the high-wing spoiler. I sat down with him for an hour or two and built the car on the computer and put in the order. I was fired up—I couldn't wait to get the car. But timing is everything, and as I mentioned, this was right before the pandemic started. A few months go by and the salesman calls me and tells me that they shut down production in Bowling Green. I was going to have to wait a little longer for the car. More time goes by. Still no car. Then I get pushed out to a 2021 model. Still no car.

At this point it had been more than a year; my dream of owning an affordable Ferrari was going out the window. I went down to the Chevy dealership to give the guy a piece of my mind.

When I got there, one of the 2020 models was sitting right there in the showroom. It was black, with red trim, but with the high-wing spoiler, just like I wanted. It wasn't blue, but this car looked even cooler. It even had matching seatbelts. The same salesman I had been talking to for over a year waved me over.

"What is this?" I asked.

It was a used car—it had 1,000 miles on it. A race car driver named Ricky Craven was flipping it for $113,000. I had a choice—pay up for this car today or wait to get one cheaper that there was no realistic chance of getting. I decided to buy the car.

I thought about financing the car. It was $113,000, after all. I didn't want to part with all that cash. I figured I'd get a five-year loan at around 2% and pay it off over the course of a year or two (later we will cover what a good rate for a car loan is). Not a bad plan.

I turned to the salesman, who was wearing a striped polo shirt, windowpane slacks, and sneakers, and told him I was interested but wanted to know my interest rate. He explained that the dealership had been in the family for three generations, and they've been serving their community since 1942, etc. Whenever you hear self-serving stuff like that you know you are about to get taken for a ride, *especially* at a dealership. I gave him my information and Mr. Salesman took me in the *back room*.

I'm sure you've had this experience before—when they start talking money, they take you in the *back room*. For someone who is not financially sophisticated, this can be a very intimidating experience. I've had people describe this stress and panic to me. This is what you call *asymmetric information*—the salesman has more information than you about the car and has more information than you about the financing options, and they are not going to let you have any of this information. You need to show up to this meeting in full battle rattle.

It's a horrible feeling when you're in the *back room*. The

salesman has power over you. You probably aren't well-educated on car loan math, and you're certainly not educated on the economics behind all the incentives.

The guy writes a number down on a piece of paper and slides it across the desk at me.

"What's that?" I asked.

"Your payment," he said.

I asked him, incredulously, "How the hell can you come up with a payment if we haven't talked about the interest rate and the maturity of the loan?" Then he started in again with the speech about how the car dealership has been serving the community since 1942, and it's been in the family for three generations.

"Dude, what is the interest rate?" I asked for the *third* time.

"Six percent," he said.

"Six percent? Are you out of your mind? What was my credit score?" He said that he got two scores and they were both above 800.

"Why am I getting a 6% loan if my credit score is above 800?" I asked.

He said that it was because *I didn't have any current car credit*—I hadn't had a car loan in ages—and because it was technically a used car, even though it only had 1,000 miles on it.

Little known fact about car dealerships—they do not make a great deal of money selling cars. They make most of their money on the financing, and also the service.

I tell him that I'll pay cash. At this point the guy was mad.

By paying cash, I was basically telling him that he wasn't going to make any money selling what was the most expensive car in the entire showroom. Most people don't understand that the car selling business isn't all that great, but the car *financing* business is amazing. Sucks for him. I wasn't about to pay 6% interest.

I bought the car and drove it off the lot and haven't seen windowpane pants guy since.

Now, paying cash for the car was not my plan. I wanted to finance it, and pay it off over the course of a year or two. I didn't want $100,000 going out the door all at once. But before I even walked into the dealership, I knew that paying cash was a possibility, and I had the ability to do it. I even brought my checkbook. I wasn't nervous or stressed out—I came *prepared*. I was also kind of annoyed.

I'm a reasonable guy. People need to be able to make a living. People need to make a profit. But not like that. Not by taking advantage of someone's financial unsophistication. He tried to pull a fast one on one of the most knowledgeable personal finance experts in the country. Imagine what he does to everyone else!

All my experiences buying cars have been terrible. I go to battle with these salesmen, so I don't get taken advantage of. This is a zero-sum game—if the salesman is happy to do the deal, you should be unhappy.

If you're wondering how I paid $113,000 for an $80,000 car and came away feeling like I got the best of it, the 2020 Corvettes were very scarce (due to production difficulties) and were trading at a rich premium. A typical car will depreciate over time—but cars that are collector's items will *appreciate* over time. This car was the rare investment I was happy to pay for.

The goal should be to pay cash for a car. Financing cars is a last resort option. In this case, I blundered into doing something smart.

It's worth saying that if you are in the *back room* of the car dealership, you will not have the ability to negotiate the terms of the car loan. The dealership does not actually lend you the money—the financing arm of the manufacturer does, or some third-party lender. If the dealership offers you a particular loan with a particular interest rate, that is typically all that is available.

There's one exception: if you are offered a seven or eight-year loan, you usually have the ability to negotiate a loan with a shorter term, like five years. *You should never have a car loan with a duration of more than five years.*

When you set foot in a car dealership, know that you are taking your life in your hands. And there are no rules. They will get you in that car. They will do whatever it takes to get you in that car, up to and including illegal sales tactics. They don't care if the car gets repossessed in four months—all they care about is making the sale.

Lucky for you, I do care, and I'm here to help mitigate the damage.

Here's my step-by-step guide to buying a car.

A step-by-step guide to buying a car

STEP ONE: CAR LOANS AND YOU

First, let's talk about cars for a moment—they're more expensive than ever.

Cars have been getting more expensive over time, for a bunch of reasons. The main one is that the government is imposing so many safety and emissions requirements, which is increasing the price of a car. For example, the backup camera in your car is worth about $800. Multiply that times by 17 million cars sold in the U.S. and we're spending $13.6 billion a year on backup cameras. Is that worth a handful of dummies not getting run over in their driveways? Those are questions for Gregory Stock, PhD to answer. The point is, if left to their own devices, people would want the option of an affordable car that gets them from A to B, rather than this computerized, overpriced, turbo supermobile. Bring back the Yugo.

Since cars are more expensive—much more expensive—they're nearly impossible to buy without financing. Therefore, my first suggestion is to familiarize yourself with how car loans work.

They are a bit like mortgages—there's principal and interest payments, and they amortize over time. And remember, like a house, buy a car that you can afford. You can prepay the principal and shorten the duration of the loan. The terms for car loans have been getting *longer* over time, as cars have gotten more expensive. My first car loan out of college was five years. Now, six, seven, eight, and even nine-year car loans are common. Cars have become so expensive that people need the longer-duration loans for the payment to be affordable. But the problem with longer loans is that you end up paying more interest over time, and interest is unproductive. And since you're paying more interest, that's more profits for the bank. Terrific.

Again: *Do not get a car loan longer than five years.* If you can't afford the car with a five-year loan, *then don't get the car;* get a cheaper car.

Savvy people don't get eight-year car loans at 6% interest. It's not a habit of highly effective people. I can tell you what will stress you out—having a giant car payment eight years from now when the car is on its last legs. I can tell you what will eliminate stress—having that car payment disappear after five years, and then you'll have all this additional cash flow.

Now, there were two times in my life when I got a car loan. The first was in college—the service academies offered this deal where first-class cadets could get a car loan and buy a car. I bought a $13,000 Toyota Tercel, new, in 1995. I had that car for eight years and racked up a bunch of miles on it.

The payment was siphoned out of my pay statement. I had completely forgotten about it, until four years later, I had paid off the loan and suddenly I had all this free cash flow—which made me realize the value of not having debt. Extra cash flow.

The second time I got a car loan was in 2010, when I bought a Toyota Highlander for $32,000. I didn't want to hand over $32,000 in cash—a good chunk of money—and decided to get a car loan from USAA: a five-year loan at 4% interest. I never made any prepayments on the loan. At the end, I added up all the interest payments I had made over five years, and it came out to $8,000. I paid $8,000 in interest for no reason whatsoever. That was a dumb decision. If you have the money to pay cash for the car, pay cash for the car.

Another thing I should mention: you do have the ability to refinance your car loan. But it's unlike refinancing a mortgage— you refinance a mortgage when interest rates go down. You refinance a car loan when your credit improves. If you had a low credit score and you got a car loan with a high interest rate, you may be eligible to refinance if your credit score has gone up significantly. This can knock a couple of hundred bucks off your payment. If you find yourself in this situation, it is worth doing.

I cannot stress to you enough the importance of having a car loan that is fair and manageable. There are people out there— and I know this for certain—who have $2,000 a month of after-tax income and an $800 car payment. Other countries don't do this. Just the U.S. The risk is not that you default on the car loan and the car is repossessed. The risk is that you actually *pay it off;* that you allow this loan to suck up all your available free cash flow, leaving no money for anything else.

Most people don't like austerity, but many people are experiencing *forced austerity* from having fixed debt charges that are too large relative to their income. They're buying the generic brand toilet paper, clipping coupons, constantly thinking about what to budget and where to cut costs, because everything goes to the car. That's not happiness.

There are a lot of people in the U.S. who are living paycheck to paycheck, and worrying about how they are going to make ends meet every month. And it's a terrible feeling—that's how you lose sleep, wondering every month, "How the hell am I going to pay the bills again?" Oftentimes, this is a direct result of accumulating too much debt—too big of a mortgage, too many student loans, and crucially, too big of a car loan. This stress can be entirely avoided. Get a car you can afford so that you have the option to pay the loan off early.

It's just a car. It's transportation. It's not who you are as a person.

STEP TWO: KNOW YOUR WORTH; DO YOUR RESEARCH

Car dealerships are designed to manipulate your emotions. Go to the dealership when you can, not when you have to. There is something about the environment—the smell, the clothes, the muzak—that makes you want to buy a car. People go into dealerships with no intention of buying a car, and they end up buying a car. It happens all the time. Buying a car is the third-most important financial decision you will make, and it must be made with forethought and deliberation. Keep in mind that you don't have to buy the car—at least, you don't want to *let on* that you have to buy a car.

The first thing you want to do before you go into the car dealership is a little homework. Know what your trade-in is worth and know what the new car is worth. This is simple enough: start by googling the make and model of your car. You'll get numbers from *Kelley's Blue Book* or similar websites. Generally, these estimates of the value of your car are consistent, and identical to the numbers that the dealership is using. "Doing research" on a car should only take you a couple of minutes—look up the value of the old car and the new car, and you're good to go. If the new car costs $40,000, and your trade-in is worth $9,000, then the transaction should cost you $31,000, before warranties and stuff like that. If it doesn't, then you know something is off, and you have to speak up. If the numbers are off—if the dealership lowballs you on the value of your trade-in—ask questions. "Why am I getting less for my trade-in? What are these extra charges?" Study the invoice and ask questions.

If you live in a highly populated area, you might have the luxury of having more than one car dealership nearby, and you can compare quotes. Not where I live. There is one Toyota dealership, and the next-closest one is two hours away. Besides, the advertised price on the dealer website is not the most important factor you should be considering. That should be how aggressive the salesman will be. And you won't know that until you actually go to the dealership.

Do not let these guys intimidate you. There's always an intimidation factor when you're the rookie walking into an unfamiliar environment; meanwhile, the other guy is a seasoned veteran. Car salesmen have extensive training on sales techniques in order to extract as much value as possible out of a car. But don't be intimidated—these guys are complete coneheads; you can outsmart any of their "techniques" by simply asking questions.

While negotiating for a car, people generally have all kinds of questions, but they don't speak up out of fear. You *must* speak up. There's no such thing as a stupid question. Only good things will come from asking questions—peace of mind and relief to your financial situation. In my negotiation for the Corvette, there was a line item on the invoice for $800 with no explanation. I asked what it was for—insurance on my keys in case I lost them. I said, "I'm not going to lose my keys, please take that off there." And I saved $800.

The other thing about negotiation is that you have to be prepared to walk away. The last thing you want is to have your *heart set* on a car—to fall in love with a car—which is also true of houses.

Times have changed. The days when you could say, "I'm outta here," and walk out the door and have these guys chase after you are over. But if you aren't satisfied with the answer, you absolutely should walk away. Because if you don't, you're going to end up with an expensive car that will destroy your finances for years. You'll be cursing yourself every time the payment is withdrawn from your bank account. You can wait a few weeks. The car will be there when you get back. And if it's not, no big deal.

Speaking as a trader, you cannot get too sentimental about material goods—everything is a trade. If you're getting a bad deal, you must walk away. The consequences of not walking away are severe. You'll end up in an $80,000 SUV with an eight-year loan at $1,000 a month. That honeymoon phase you felt between you and the car—it's over. Now the car owns you for all your worth.

There are some personal finance experts out there who tell people to *always* get cheaper, used cars. I get it. But this may end up costing you more money in the long run—if you pay $8,000 for a lemon, and it starts breaking down all the time, it will cost you more in maintenance than what you paid for the car. Which kind of defeats the purpose of getting a used car. My whole thing with Toyotas is based on the idea that Toyotas (the engine, at least) never break down. It wasn't a fancy car, but it got me from A to B. And if you get a Toyota (or a Honda, or a Hyundai), and you buy it new, you're going to be able to drive that car for ten years without any mechanical problems.

STEP THREE: KNOW YOUR ENEMY

Being a car salesman is a funny sort of job. It doesn't require a college degree, even though salesmen are handling large transactions with lots of money and complex financing. All it requires is an underdeveloped conscience that is not too squeamish about taking advantage of people. The goal is to become more sophisticated than the car salesman.

You've heard all the mental tricks that casinos play on gamblers, with the absence of clocks, the busy carpets, and the ringing of slot machines. A car dealership is not too different. When you walk into a car dealership, what is the first thing that you notice? The smell. That new car smell, man. They should take that stuff and put it in a bottle and sell it as perfume. It would work every time. My Corvette, a little over a year later, still has that new car smell. It is glorious.

The other thing you will notice is that salesmen are making an effort to look nice. Not suits, per se, but they're wearing button-downs or nice polo shirts with slacks. You wouldn't take them seriously if they were wearing cargo shorts with a flat-bill cap, though that is probably what they wear in their spare time.

Here is what the salesman knows: he knows exactly how much profit accrues to the dealership if he sells the car at a certain price point, and he knows exactly how much profit accrues to the dealership if he sells the car with various financing or warranty packages. Unfortunately, I do not have that information. What I do know is that what is good for the dealership is not good for me. If the salesman is steering you one way, you had better go the other.

Talk to a car salesman sometime. I know some personally. They will confirm what I am telling you—they will do *whatever it takes* to sell a car. Above and beyond the usual stuff, where they have you sit in the car and sniff the new car smell, and then they lean over the driver's side window and ask you if you like it. No, I'm not talking about psychological tricks like that. I'm talking about the stuff that goes on in the *back room*, where they slide a piece of paper across the desk and expect you to just accept that payment. If the problem here is *asymmetric information*, the goal is to make the information a little less asymmetric. Familiarize yourself with the information, with the salesmen, to minimize the damage.

Depending on where you are in the country, you might see these fleabag car dealerships along the side of the road. Where I live, there are a lot of them. Stay very far away. These car dealerships sell cheap used cars to subprime borrowers, and often saddle them with loans that charge 20% interest or more. You could pay $3,000 for a car and end up paying $8,000 in interest. The more likely scenario is that you'll default on the loan. I would guess that the vast majority of cars sold at the fleabag auto dealerships get repossessed. The repo industry has become very efficient over the years. There are documented instances where if you miss your monthly payment by one day, there is an electronic device on the ignition that prevents the car from starting. You really don't want to be eating dinner when a tow truck pulls up and drags the car out of your driveway.

The problem is that the only thing people know to ask about is the payment. What is the monthly? The salesman slides a piece of paper across the desk with a number on it and says, "Does that work?" And if people figure they can make the payment work within their budget, then they'll foolishly agree to it, without doing the math on how much interest they are paying. This happens at the fleabag car dealerships, and it happens at the big, fancy car dealerships. It seems as though nobody cares about the actual rate of interest. You should. This may change, but in the current interest rate environment, **if you are offered a car**

loan with an interest rate higher than 6%, you should not take it. Get a cheaper, used car, and pay cash for it.

If you're wondering how all these sleazy car salesmen can get away with this, it's because they're unregulated. That's right—car dealerships successfully lobbied the government to be exempt from Dodd-Frank, the law regulating the financial industry that was passed after the Great Financial Crisis. So there are virtually no consumer protections. The Consumer Financial Protection Bureau has no jurisdiction over car dealerships. It's the Wild West.

The most effective kind of regulation requires disclosure. Salesmen at car dealerships should be required by law to tell you the interest rate and duration of a car loan, instead of just the payment. They should be required to go over every line item on the invoice. We've done it with other industries—the credit card industry got overhauled in 2009, and now they have to disclose how long it will take to pay off your balance if you just make the minimum payment. There are a lot of bad actors selling cars. There are good people, for sure, but the incentives are so misaligned that they are assured of not acting in your best interest. Never bring a knife to a gunfight.

STEP FOUR: DEPRECIATION AND YOU

Everyone knows that cars depreciate. Most people don't understand the full implications of that.

If you take out a mortgage on your house, you're borrowing against an asset that has a good chance of increasing in value. If you take out a loan to buy a car, you're borrowing against an asset that will one day go to zero. It's not a good system.

If you get an eight-year loan, here is what could happen: the car could go bang in year six, and then you will have to make payments on a car that you don't own for two years. Or you will take the existing loan and roll it into a new loan—a big, giant loan—and you will be making payments on two cars while you only own one. You might have a $60,000 loan on a $40,000 car. It doesn't take a genius to see why that is not a good idea.

Not only do cars depreciate, but they also depreciate on a curve. They depreciate very fast in the beginning, and then taper off toward the end. That old saying about how a car is worth $3,000 less when you drive it off the lot is absolutely true. But if you have a car loan and you pay it off in five years, and then you own the car for ten, 12, 15 years, that's the best thing in the world. The car is hardly depreciating at that point and you can drive it forever for free.

Another rule of thumb that I have is that you should spend no more than 10% of your income on transportation. Easy enough for people living in a city, using public transportation. The rest of us have to do math on cars. The average person will spend about $3,000 a year on gas, dependent on how many miles they drive and what gas prices are, of course. Then you factor in how much insurance you are paying on your car—say, $1,200, for example.

Now you have to figure out depreciation. If you have a $40,000 car and you plan to own it for ten years, if you use straight-line depreciation, that comes out to $4,000 a year. Maybe you want to throw in $500 for service. So the cost to own the car—including gas, insurance, depreciation, and service—comes out to $7,700 a year. This means that you can only own this car if you make $77,000 a year, in order to keep your transportation costs under 10% of your income.

It's important to keep transportation costs less than 10% of your income, for the same reason that you want to keep your housing costs less than 25% of your income. If it's higher than that, it's going to crowd out other financial goals, like saving for retirement. The people I know who have three or four expensive cars have a lot of money going out the door in transportation expenses. Not coincidentally, these are not people who are saving for retirement. It's all free cash flow to cars.

The average price of a new car in the U.S. is now over $46,000. Nine out of ten cars are financed in the U.S. These are terrible statistics. It's not my place to be harsh on people who take out car loans. I get it. I wish people didn't have to take out debt to buy a car, but this is where we are. The alternative is that you're driving a 26-year-old Ford Exploder that's about to break down at any moment. This is one of these situations in life where we bend over and buy the new car. But there are ways to minimize the damage.

STEP FIVE: CONSIDER ALTERNATIVES—LEASING OR RIDE-SHARING SERVICES

German cars have a not-so-good reputation when it comes to reliability. As someone once explained to me, those cars are *leasing* cars, because they start having problems after about three years.

I don't want to spend a great deal of time on leasing, other than to tell you that in most cases, it's a profoundly bad deal. The math behind it is a little complex, so I will leave it out. The thing that makes leases attractive is that the monthly payments are typically lower than a car loan. This is flypaper for idiots. Because at the end of the lease, you don't own the car; where if you did, you could sell the car and get cash, or trade it in for something else. A lease is like a loan, and the implied interest rate can be very high—it averages around 14%. So you are still paying interest, whether you realize it or not.

People like leasing cars because they get a new car every three years. Sure, that's fun. But it's a luxury that most people cannot afford. Not to mention that whenever you lease a car, there are mileage restrictions and other rules—no fun when you use up all the allotted miles and you end up taking Ubers around.

I do want to mention Uber briefly. A lot of people think of Uber as an internet taxi company—it is more than that. The purpose of Uber is to increase the capacity utilization of a car. Think of this: You drive a car to work, and it sits in the parking lot. You drive it home, and it sits in your driveway. Probably, you're not carrying any passengers in the car. The average car has a 4% capacity utilization. A car that had a 100% capacity utilization would be driving 24 hours a day, filled with passengers.

The way we use cars now is very inefficient, leaving them sitting in parking lots. A better way to do it would be to have fewer cars on the road but driving all the time with multiple passengers. *That* is the purpose of Uber—not a taxi company.

The problem with Uber is that the economics only made sense when it was a startup, and was receiving billions in funding, which it was using to subsidize rides. Once Uber became a public company, and had to turn a profit, the prices went up, making it not as economical for consumers.

However, when you add up all the costs of owning a car, including insurance and depreciation, it can work out more expensive than taking Ubers around. Think of it this way: if you had $7,200 in transportation costs a year, if you spent $20 a day on Uber, it would end up being about a push. I don't think we've heard the last of Uber (and Lyft). The point here is that if you're considering using Uber all the time instead of buying a car, depending on where you live, that might not be a bad idea.

In conclusion:
life is a highway

New cars don't break down. Toyotas, Hondas, and Hyundais don't break down. Get something like a Toyota Yaris, a Honda Civic, and finance it for five years at 4% or less. Drive it for ten to 15 years. Drive it into the ground. That is the best way I know to beat the car game. Incidentally, these cars tend to hold their value very well—you will be able to do well upon trade-in.

I can tell you the surefire way to lose the car game: buy a $80,000 Chevy Silverado that's so big you have to do a 19-point turn to back it into a parking space. Maybe I don't understand big truck culture—or maybe I do. Nowadays, these are not working trucks—these are luxury vehicles. And if you wouldn't buy an $80,000 Maserati, then don't buy an $80,000 truck. Nobody is fooled by your pathetic attempts at blue-collar sensibilities. I look at an $80,000 truck and I see a 600 credit score. If you're going to be hauling logs, that's one thing; but nobody drives their trucks like you see in the commercials. You don't want your car payment to be bigger than your house payment.

The funny thing about buying a car is that it's designed to be stressful. If it's not stressful, the salesman isn't doing his job. But it's just a matter of preparation, and the preparation takes a couple of minutes. You must have the willingness to speak up—and not let the salesman put you in a loan that is not in your best interests.

Another good idea: put a down payment on the car, much like you would on a house, and have some equity from the start. One hundred percent financing is never a good idea—on anything. Think of it this way: you're fighting over $3,000.

That's the extra profit that the salesman is trying to extract from you, and that's the amount you're trying to save. $3,000 is a decent amount of money. That's the difference between taking a vacation, or not.

It would be nice if we didn't have to waste any thought on buying a car or dealing with bozo salesmen. But we do, because buying more car than you can afford is one of the number one ways to tomahawk yourself financially. In the end it will cause all kinds of unnecessary stress—you'll be emotionally drained wondering how to make the payments. Cars keep getting more expensive, new and used. If what you're doing seems a little extravagant, it probably is. If you can do without an expensive car, there is so much more you will be able to afford—or save.

The definition of freedom is having a car that is paid for. You know anyone with a car that is paid for? Ask them what it's like. Then drive off into the sunset with nothing but the open road and the notion of stress-free living ahead of you (except for maybe a few idiots on the road).

Congratulations—we have now completed our discussion on debt. Now we are moving onto *risk*—particularly risk in the financial markets.

....

PART IV

Risk
Stress

······································

CHAPTER 12

Risk Is a Source of Stress

Lf you've done everything right so far, you have the right attitude toward money, you are free of debt stress, and you are building up a pile of money. Congratulations.

What are you going to do with it?

Invest it, obviously. That's what we're here to talk about.

How I got started in investing

Somewhere along the way, you have probably heard someone refer to investing as "having your money work for you." They have some mutual funds in a 401(k) and this magically spits out returns that are considerably better than what you would get in a bank account.

This happened to me in 1997. I was stationed on a Coast Guard cutter, and one time, when we went to sea, we pulled into San Diego for fuel. My fellow officer Adam leaves and goes to one of those old newspaper vending machines, and gets a newspaper. He opens it to the money section.

"What are you doing?" I asked him.

"I'm checking on my mutual funds," he said.

"What's a mutual fund?" I asked.

I thought the only way you could invest was in a bank account. I was getting 5% in a bank account at the time, which was nothing to sneeze at, but my friend Adam was making much more.

That literally was the beginning of my financial journey. I was so motivated by *greed* that I had to learn about this world where you could make 15% or 20% a year on your money.

I learned that mutual funds are a pool of money collected from investors to invest in a portfolio of stocks on their behalf. The shares in the mutual fund are a proportional interest in that portfolio. If the stocks go up, you make money, and if the stocks go down, you lose money.

And that's the thing with mutual funds—you are exposed to potential loss. Unlike a bank account, where there is no risk to principal and you are FDIC insured. I probably have an above-average risk appetite, and I was willing to accept losses in the pursuit of gains. The context is that it was the late 1990s, and stocks pretty much went straight up during the late 1990s.

I set out to pick some mutual funds. I did some reading on index funds, and how it is very difficult for a portfolio manager to beat the return of an index. That sounded intriguing to me. But I wanted to give stock-picking a chance, too, so I picked some actively managed mutual funds. One of them was a very old and boring value fund, with cheap stocks that paid big dividends. That ended up being my best investment over the next ten years.

In 1999, I started trading individual stocks. I opened up an Ameritrade account, and put a few thousand bucks in it. I had no illusions about what I was doing—I was just screwing around. I wanted to see if I could make a few hundred bucks here and there. And for the next few years, I had mostly winning trades and a few losing ones. It didn't add up to much money, but I was experimenting, and I learned a lot. In fact, you learn *real fast* when you put your own capital at risk.

But like I said, I did occasionally experience losses. Not catastrophic, but occasionally I would lose a few months of spending money. The losses were painful. When you make an investment, you don't *intend* to lose money. You obviously think the trade you are putting on will be a winner. But sometimes you miscalculate, and sometimes you are overcome by events, and sometimes you have just plain bad luck. Nobody plans on losing money. Sometimes you send a bunch of cash to your mutual funds and you get rinsed in a bear market which was completely out of your control.

Thinking about risk

Since we are talking about losing money, you have to think of the *probability* of losing money and how much you will lose when you do.

If you're investing in broad stock market mutual funds, you have about a 48% chance of losing money in one day, and a 26% chance of losing money in one year. The average annual gain of the stock market over time, depending on how you calculate it, is about 9%. Sometimes it makes much more than that, and sometimes it gets creamed. What you are really concerned with is the *risk* of the investment.

Risk can be loosely translated as *volatility*, or how much something moves around. A bank account effectively has a volatility of zero. It doesn't move. A bond moves a little more than that, but not much. Stocks move around quite a bit, depending on what kind of stocks you have. Tech stocks move more than banks, for instance. And bitcoin moves most of all. When you buy a stock or any other investment, you should first think about the asset's volatility. Because the more risk you take, the more *stress* it is going to cause you.

Risk is proportional to stress.

The problem is that risk is also generally proportional to returns. You can save yourself a lot of stress by investing in bonds, but you probably won't make very much money. You could potentially earn a lot by investing in tech stocks, but the volatility could give you a heart attack. The key here is to find the level of risk that you are comfortable with.

This is one of my objections to index funds, because when you invest in an index, *not only do you get the returns of the index, but you also get the volatility of the index.* The S&P 500 index is pretty volatile. On average, it moves about 1% per day. It crashes occasionally. In the Great Depression, the stock market went down 89%. You might think that could never happen again, but it absolutely could happen again. There is no rule that says it can't. Stocks go down. Stocks crash.

Stocks have also been the best way for Americans to build wealth for over a century. But the projections for the next 100 years may not come to pass if the conditions that were present for the last 100 years no longer hold true. Stupid example, but stocks would stop going up if the U.S. became a communist country. We would no longer have a stock market! The one thing I constantly tell people is that *anything can happen.* Stuff that is beyond our imagination can happen.

There is risk in everything we do, whether we realize it or not. And sometimes we are not so good at perceiving and evaluating risks. If you had any idea how dangerous getting in a car was, you would never do it. Conversely, people freak out about letting their kids walk to school. Do you know how many children are abducted by strangers in the United States every year? One hundred and fifteen. One every three days, approximately, in the entire country. It's more probable that you'll be struck by lightning.

We think that small risks are big and big risks are small. In the capital markets, we tend to think that big risks are small; and in the *housing market*, when you buy a house, you really think that big risks are small. But we think that small risks are big, like getting bitten by a shark while swimming in the ocean. It is a one-in-a-trillion shot. But everyone saw *Jaws*, so we are afraid of sharks.

There is risk in everything we do. Nobody thought there was any risk in money market mutual funds in 2008, but those almost went tapioca in the Great Financial Crisis.

There is no foolproof way to avoid financial risk in your life. You could keep your money in the bank, but maybe all the banks go bankrupt and FDIC croaks as well. You could take your money out of the bank, and keep it under the mattress, but you could get robbed, and you are losing money due to inflation. You could keep your money in T-bills, but one day the federal government may decide not to pay. You could just buy gold and keep that in your house, but you could get robbed there too, and the price of gold fluctuates over time. There is no escaping financial risk. Even the safest places to put your money, like Treasury bills or gold, have risk. It is inescapable. If you're really paranoid, you can build a portfolio of all these safe haven assets—but it won't return very much. You just have to be smart about risk and hope for the best.

I say "be smart about it" because in recent years, people have not been so smart about it. Crypto, for example. Not only did the price of bitcoin go down a lot, but if that wasn't enough, a few exchanges went bankrupt and customer funds disappeared. Even outside of crypto, there have been some instances where blue-chip stocks went down 90% or more. Peloton seemed like a sure bet, but it pulled forward about five years of demand, and almost went bankrupt. GE has been around for over 100 years, but eventually got kicked out of the Dow after a decade of mismanagement.

Risk management is about fighting your emotions. If I could summarize it in one sentence, my philosophy of risk management is as follows: *This too shall pass.*

If you're losing money on your portfolio, and all hope is lost, *this too shall pass*. Things will get better. And if you're making so much money that you're running around telling your friends how you're killing it in the stock market, *this too shall pass.*

Oftentimes, the best thing to do is to not look at your portfolio. Just don't log in. Live your life and forget about it.

When you check your portfolio balance, there is some likelihood of getting *negative feedback*. If you go in your phone and look at your account, and it is down, you will feel sad. If you go in your phone and look at your account and it is up, you feel happy. If your account is down, you will experience negative thoughts—you will think that you are a failure and you suck at investing and you might as well just liquidate your account. Of course, that would be the worst thing you can possibly do—you have to stay invested and let the gains continue to compound.

There is some research that shows that more information, consumed more frequently, leads to bad decision-making. The people who read newsletters and watch financial TV don't tend to make better financial decisions than the people who don't. In fact, they frequently make worse decisions. You might find this hard to believe, but in my professional life, writing an investment newsletter, I try to consume as little information as possible, because it affects my emotions, and influences my decision-making. I can't tell you the last time I watched financial TV—usually only if it is on in an airport lounge.

If you think about it, the ideal investment would be one that goes up 8% a year with no volatility—kind of like a savings account in 1984. But these days, if you want to get 8% returns, you have to take some risk, which means you will have good years and bad years. The cumulative effect of a bunch of good years and bad years is a lot of stress. This book tells you practical ways to mitigate that risk and also practical ways to mitigate that stress.

The first and best way to protect yourself against the vagaries of the financial markets is through *diversification*.

Diversification

Diversification is the idea that you don't really know what stocks will do well and what stocks will do poorly, so you own a lot of them. Some will do well, and some will do poorly, but *on average*, they will go up. But sometimes all stocks go down, in a bear market.

So it helps to be diversified into bonds as well. But sometimes, like in 2022, stocks and bonds go down together. So it helps to own other things, like commodities. If you wanted to be *perfectly diversified* you would own a little bit of every stock, bond, commodity, and currency in the entire world. But that is impractical. So most people buy some U.S. stocks and some U.S. bonds and call it a day.

Now, the problem with diversification is that the more stocks you buy, the closer you get to becoming an index fund, and the closer you get to getting the *average* return. Some people, but not all, are content with the average return. Some people want to earn more than that. The most legendary trader of all time, the great Stan Druckenmiller, refers to diversification as "diworseification." He tries to earn super-normal returns by constructing a very concentrated portfolio. And the most concentrated portfolio you have is one stock. Some people did this with Tesla. Tesla had a cult following of investors who made that one stock practically their entire portfolio. And for a while, it paid off. Tesla made millionaires out of thousands of people. But we should not judge decisions on the basis of their results. Yes, it worked out for a while, but it might not have. And then, if they never sold, at the time of writing they are down 50% from the highs.

There are people out there who pretty much do have a one-stock portfolio—employees of companies who get compensated primarily in stock. Lehman Brothers stock was 25% of my compensation—it went to zero. People who work for banks and tech companies get a lot of stock as compensation. Sometimes it works, sometimes it doesn't. They have to spend a lot of time figuring out how to manage that risk, when one stock comprises 80% of their net worth. It's a nice problem to have, I guess. But ideally, you would want a lot more diversification than that.

The best way to achieve diversification is through a mutual fund. When you buy an S&P 500 index fund, for example, you are buying 500 stocks at once. When you own 500 stocks you are pretty much diversified. When you are buying an actively managed fund, you might be buying 100–200 stocks at once— also good diversification.

If you are investing in stocks on your own, it takes a fair amount of money to achieve good diversification. The conventional wisdom is that you can achieve diversification by owning 30 stocks. Even 30 stocks is a lot. If you had $10,000 in each one of them, that's $300,000. This is why most people who trade stocks are doing it recreationally—they're punting around four to five stocks for fun. I would not characterize that as a diversified portfolio.

There's nothing wrong with trading stocks recreationally, as long as you are being honest about your intentions. In fact, I have a theory about this: most of the investment industry is really for fun. Everyone knows what the answer is: own an index fund. But it sure is fun to try to beat the index. And when you don't, you're sure that you can do it the following year. And maybe you do beat it once in a while—but a lot of luck is involved.

If you're doing it for fun and for knowledge, it's a nice hobby. I know lots of people for whom finance is a hobby. But once you start thinking you are the second coming of Peter Lynch or

Paul Tudor Jones, that is about the point that the piano is going to fall on your head.

Sure, some people can trade for a living. They are very talented. But they represent much less than 1% of investors. I'm friendly with one of them—the great Mark Minervini, one of the most talented stock traders of all time, who dropped out of school in the eighth grade to trade full-time. He's built a very large fortune.

It's tempting to see people like Mark and think, "I can do it too," but it's simply not the case. We do not have the emotional makeup. Mark is perhaps the most unemotional trader I have met—he ruthlessly cuts losing positions, without a trace of emotion. I suppose that can be taught—to a point—but the best course of action is to just do the thing you do every day to earn that income and then punt around in your spare time. The idea that you can earn a living as a trader or an investor is very seductive, and people pursue it into the gates of insanity. I know my weaknesses and shortcomings—I'm just not cut out for it. And you probably aren't, either.

There is a personal finance guru out there who says that everyone should be 100% invested in aggressive growth mutual funds. Why? Because they return the most. And that's about the level of most people's financial sophistication these days—look for the highest return without any consideration for risk. If you were fully invested in aggressive growth mutual funds in 2000, you would have been down to the tune of 80% or more. This guru's analysis is backward-looking—these funds have returned the most in the past, therefore they will return the most in the future. It is comically simplistic.

There is no silver bullet. There is no one thing you can do throughout an investing career that will solve all your financial problems. The markets exhibit a property known as *nonstationarity*—it is like playing a game where the rules constantly change. Nothing works forever. The goal is to build a portfolio that will endure throughout every market cycle. You will sacrifice a little bit in the way of returns, while greatly reducing your risk, and consequently, your financial stress.

If you want to minimize financial stress, you should diversify. Going all-in on Tesla is not the way to go, even if it works out. You don't need to make a million percent. Put another way, if you really do make about 8% a year over your investing career, making contributions along the way, you will have a more-than-comfortable retirement, with a lot left over to do fun stuff. But even a diversified portfolio of stocks can cause you a lot of heartache. I have a solution to that, which we will discuss in Chapter 14.

Insurance

This is the point in time in which we should talk about insurance. In short—always buy it. There is a mathematical reason for this, which is too complex to explain here. But the main reason to buy insurance is to minimize financial stress.

I know some people here on the coast of South Carolina, in a hurricane zone, that do not have homeowner's insurance or flood insurance. They are rolling the dice. They own the house free and clear, with no mortgage, which means they are not required to purchase insurance. They see the insurance as an unnecessary expense. And yes, you may go a lifetime without ever needing it, but it's still a bad decision if you don't buy insurance.

Wall Street people know this: you always want to insure against catastrophic loss. You want to avoid the zero. If there is any possibility, however remote, that you can be taken to zero by the loss of your house, you should buy insurance.

And it's not just homeowner's insurance and flood insurance. You are legally required to purchase auto insurance as a precondition of driving a car; and as of 2010, you are required to purchase health insurance, or pay a penalty. *Term* life insurance is always a good idea, at a multiple of your income for a single year.

Think of it this way. If your house was destroyed by fire or hurricane, just the emotional distress as a result of losing all your treasured belongings (and maybe pets) is bad enough. The last thing you want to do is be financially ruined at the same time. It's hard to recover from something like that.

The funny thing about insurance is that lots of people purchase insurance on their life or their home, but they do not purchase it on their portfolio—which is often their biggest asset. Don't you think that's weird? This is very common: someone might have a $50,000 car and a $500,000 house, which are both insured, along with a $1m portfolio of stocks, which is not. You might not know that there are ways to insure a portfolio of stocks. That is outside the scope of this book, but just know that it can be done. And the reason a lot of people don't do it is because it can be expensive. Of course, an implicit way to buy insurance on your portfolio is to just be diversified across asset classes. See Chapter 14.

Optimism
and pessimism

There is not a lot of money to be made in being a pessimist. There is lots of money to be made in being an optimist. Think of it this way—it is very difficult to bet against human ingenuity. Yes, progress is not linear—the whole history of human advancement is one of three steps forward, two steps back. And there is a whole class of investor that is very focused on trying to profit from the two steps back. That is a very hard way to make a living—you have to have impeccable timing.

Having said that, I've found that there is a certain naivete that goes along with being an optimist. I hear this from people all the time: "The market always comes back." It sure has, over the last 100 years, but there is no rule that says that will be the case in the future. I prefer a philosophy of *cautious optimism*—you want to be positively exposed to human ingenuity, but you have to manage risk along the way, because drawdowns and pullbacks in markets can mess with your psychology. You should not be investing in stocks unless you are prepared to lose half your money—full stop. So then the question becomes: how do you mitigate risk? There are ways to do that, which we shall discuss in time.

The other problem with saying that *the market always comes back* is that yes, it generally does, but perhaps not on a timeframe that is acceptable to you. From 1929 to 1945, the market went nowhere—16 years down the tubes, with a Depression along the way. From 1969 to 1982, the market went nowhere, with one big bear market in between. If you were getting ready to retire in 2000, for example, you just lost half your retirement in two years, which is going to greatly reduce your standard of living.

This is why the conventional wisdom is that the older you get, the more exposure you should have to bonds. The old rule of thumb was that your allocation to bonds should be equal to your age. If you are 70 years old, you should have a 70% allocation to bonds. That pretty much went out the window in the bull market of the 2010s, and oldsters were loading up their portfolios with tech stocks. That's just bad risk management. But you know how it is: greed takes over, and cautious optimism goes out the window.

My experience
with risk stress

I have experienced financial risk stress twice in my life. Once, when Lehman blew up—there was not much I could do about that. A second time, when I put on a trade in enormous size, and it went against me. I lost about 25% of my net worth. The story has a happy ending—I held on and eventually made all my money back and then some. But it was terrible risk management. And it pretty much ruined all of 2017 for me. I was a nervous wreck. If I could do it all over again, I would have appropriately sized the trade and saved myself all the heartache. I would have made *less money*, but it would have been worth it. Financial stress is the worst. And risk stress is the worst kind of financial stress, because it is avoidable. All of these disasters are man-made. We do it to ourselves. And it is completely unnecessary.

I have spent a 24-year career in the financial markets. It was my ambition to become a trader—to take risk. I don't enjoy it anymore. The idea of trying to make a living by trading sounds like the worst thing in the world. Too much stress. The reason people do this is simple: money won is sweeter than money earned. There is nothing glamorous about being a working stiff, going to work every day and earning a paycheck. Knife-fighting in the capital markets, on the other hand, is worthy of admiration and respect. And so everyone fancies themselves as a trader. I have seen a few iterations of this—in 1998–2000 and 2020–2022, in the bubbliest bull markets in history. Trading was *easy*, but that's an anomaly—trading is only easy for very brief periods in history. It is a slog and should be left to the professionals.

When I was running ETF trading at Lehman Brothers, I was

a basket case. I had developed very serious obsessive-compulsive disorder, involving highly ritualized behavior around locking doors and turning off my computer. I had a level of anxiety that most people never experience—I was basically operating in a state of sheer terror 24 hours a day. That takes a toll on you, after a while. When Lehman went bankrupt, and I set out on my own, all the symptoms disappeared. I could finally relax. My life got infinitely better.

Some people are risk-seeking—they are gamblers. They crave financial risk. Some people bet on sports, some people play blackjack, and others get their fix in the financial markets. Others become venture capitalists or entrepreneurs. They don't feel "normal" unless they are taking risk. We need people like that. The economy grows because of the actions of crazy gamblers. I'm just not cut out for it, and there is a good chance that you aren't, either. We won't get to be billionaires. And that is okay. What we trade away in the form of unlimited upside, we get back in peace and serenity.

I wouldn't trade places with Elon Musk. I said that on Twitter once, and I got roasted. Who wouldn't want to be one of the richest people in the world? Half the country loves him, half the country hates him, he's constantly being fricasseed online, being chased by lawyers, and threatened by politicians who want to put him out of business, or worse. He has a bunch of children with several different mothers. Who needs it?

That is a path I would not choose for myself, or anyone I care about. This is where Achilles says, "That is why no one will remember your name." There are no solutions, only trade-offs. As I've said before in this book, there are two possible paths: the path that will make you the most money, and the path that will bring you the most happiness. I am an expert on the latter.

But in the next chapter, we will focus on making money, as I teach you the very basics on investing.

CHAPTER 13

Investment Basics

I have to teach you everything about the financial markets in a few pages. Better get started.

I will add that this chapter is purely educational, and that it gets a bit complex at times. If you start feeling a bit confused, the good news is that by the time we get to the end of the chapter, we will dispense with the complexity and introduce my methodology for simple, diversified investing.

I want to begin with something boring, but it's for your own good.

The Federal Reserve. Perhaps you have heard of it.

The Federal Reserve

People scream and yell and riot in the street about who is going to be president. Which is weird, because the president is *not* the most powerful person in the country. The chairman of the Federal Reserve is.

The Federal Reserve is a bank. It is the central bank. The bank in charge of all the banks. It does a lot of things, like regulation and clearing checks, but crucially, it sets monetary policy for the United States. That means that it sets the money supply—how much money is in the economy—and also the level of interest rates. But not all interest rates—just an interest rate known as the Federal funds interest rate, which is the rate that banks charge when they lend to each other on an overnight basis. But by setting the Fed funds rate, the Fed can influence all other interest rates, as many rates, like the prime rate, are benchmarked off of Fed funds.

There are 19 main Fed officials—the seven members of the Board of Governors in Washington, DC, and the 12 regional Federal Reserve Bank presidents, in various cities around the country. The seven governors are political appointees, and must be confirmed by the Senate; the 12 regional presidents are not. Eight times a year, a subset of 12 of these Fed officials meet in Washington to discuss monetary policy. After the meeting, they issue a directive which determines actions on interest rates and other things, then go have a beer.

The Fed has two mandates: price stability, and employment. Which is to say that it's supposed to fight inflation (or even deflation), and the Fed wants as many people to have jobs as possible. These goals are in conflict with each other, and both are political third rails.

I will cut to the chase: you have probably heard that the

Federal Reserve is printing money. This is true. Up until early 2022, they were actively printing money—on purpose. They thought that printing money would help the economy. Well, any idiot knows that if you print money, and you have more money chasing the same amount of goods, we will experience inflation, and that is exactly what happened. Printing money has caused the price of milk and beef and lumber and steel to go up, but it also caused the price of *assets* to go up: houses and stocks and bonds. It is mostly the Fed's fault. If you can't afford to buy a house, now you know why.

The history on this is that during the Great Financial Crisis, the Fed thought we were going into a depression. They lowered rates to zero, but since you can't lower rates below zero, they decided to print money as well—they called it *quantitative easing*. This is when they print money to buy U.S. treasury bonds, which has the effect of lowering interest rates across maturities. So not only was the Fed influencing short-term rates, it was influencing long-term rates as well, bringing them down, so people could more easily borrow money for houses and cars and things. Quantitative easing may have been successful in preventing a recession from getting worse, but the Fed kept doing it long after it was necessary. They stopped for a while, and then started again during the pandemic. Then inflation happened.

When you start to get inflation, the Fed is supposed to *raise* interest rates, which causes the economy to slow down, and stops inflation in its tracks. But there is no president, no senator, no politician who wants the Fed to raise rates and cause a recession in an election year. So the Fed is sometimes held hostage to political concerns. They're not supposed to be—the Fed is independent from the government—but as we've seen in recent years, the Fed has lost most of its independence.

The other thing about zero interest rates is that while it might be great for borrowers, it's terrible for savers. In ye olde

1984, you used to be able to get 8% interest in a bank account. And if you could get 8% interest in a bank account, investing in stocks is pointless. So when the Fed lowers interest rates to zero, and savings accounts don't yield anything, it forces people to take more and more risk: buying bonds, buying stocks. Retirees and people who live on a fixed income are especially harmed. Grandma and grandpa have to buy risky junk bonds just to get some kind of income that they can live off of. It's a bad situation. Zero rates have all kinds of negative externalities. But it should be no surprise that the stock market has gone straight up.

The Fed is the most powerful institution in government, and can affect your daily life in a way that no other branch of the government can. And yet most people are completely ignorant of the Fed and how it works. I talk about it with people, and their eyes glaze over. And for sure, central bankers are profoundly boring people. But there have been various central banks in history that have made things very exciting for their citizens, and not in a good way. Not to editorialize too much, but I'm not sure why we allow the most important price in our economy—the price of money—to be manipulated by a bunch of unelected bureaucrats. Leave it to the market.

The business cycle

The economy theoretically has a business cycle. There is an expansion phase, where the economy is growing, and a recession phase, where the economy is shrinking.

The nature of the business cycle has changed in the last 20 or so years. In the past, we had a fairly regular business cycle, with frequent booms and busts; and now, we have a very prolonged boom phase, punctuated by the occasional crisis. None of the last three recessions are what I would characterize as "normal"—they were all accompanied by a crash in the stock market. This has implications for how you invest.

It's important to have some knowledge of the business cycle as you go through your daily life. On a very personal level, you may lose your job. You may not think it is possible for you to lose your job, but you may, in fact, lose your job.

So if there is some likelihood that you might lose your job, how does that affect how you manage your financial affairs? We covered this earlier—have an emergency fund worth six to 12 months of expenses. Sure, you will probably get unemployment benefits, and sure, you might get them for a really long time (because it is politically unpalatable to kick people off of unemployment benefits during a recession), but it doesn't mean you shouldn't prepare. You should always be financially self-sufficient. Never, ever count on a bailout from someone else.

You should at least have a working knowledge of how we measure the health of the economy. The U.S. has hundreds of different economic statistics. Most of them are calculated by the BLS, or Bureau of Labor Statistics, which is in the Commerce Department.

The big ones to know are the employment numbers, CPI (Consumer Price Index), GDP (Gross Domestic Product), and some of the manufacturing surveys. The unemployment rate is probably at the front of most Americans' minds. At the time of writing, the unemployment rate is very low. It got up to 10% during the 2007–08 financial crisis, and it got higher than that during the pandemic. For context, it got up to *twenty-five freaking percent* during the Great Depression. Usually, when it gets over 6%, people start squealing.

Let's now talk about the basics of investing.

The basics
of investing

WHAT IS A STOCK?

A stock represents ownership in a company. Even if you only have one share of Apple, out of the billions of shares outstanding, you are an owner of Apple. And periodically, certain matters will be voted on at shareholder meetings, and you can vote your share. Not like it would make any difference, because there are institutional investors with millions of shares, but you can, even though it is mostly symbolic.

If you're buying the stock of a company through your brokerage app or whatever, you are buying shares of a *public* company. Any company that offers shares to the public has to do certain things. Mostly, it has to submit to regulation by the Securities and Exchange Commission; and it has to publish periodic financial statements. There are about 3,000 public companies in the United States.

There are lots of companies that aren't public—they are, naturally, private. They don't have to publish periodic financial statements. The idea is that the facts of a corporation should be disclosed to individual investors, and if someone owns part of a private company, they are probably rich and don't need protection. You have probably heard of an IPO—that is where a private company offers shares to the public for the first time.

Stocks trade on an exchange. This used to be simple. In the old days, a listed stock traded on the New York Stock Exchange (NYSE), and everything else traded on NASDAQ. They were two very different exchanges. The NYSE was a specialist system—basically, one guy having a monopoly on trading a stock; and the NASDAQ had a market-maker system—dozens of banks and brokers making competitive markets. Guess which one was better? Anyway, over time, exchanges have proliferated. Last I heard there were about 17 of them, most of them electronic, and the market share of the NYSE had dipped to under 10%.

When you submit an order through your brokerage app it can get routed practically anywhere, and there is a high likelihood that you will be trading against a computer. The market microstructure in the U.S. is fantastically complicated. But it's good—we have deep, liquid markets, and execution quality is generally excellent. I would spend precisely zero time thinking about if you are getting ripped off on your stock trades. I would spend more time thinking about whether your mutual fund is getting ripped off on its stock trades.

So why buy a stock?

The classic answer is that you think the company will earn more money, and this will be rewarded by the market in terms of a higher stock price. But oftentimes, companies whose earnings are growing don't see their stocks rise very much; and oftentimes, companies that don't earn money at all, or lose money, see their stock prices explode. If you read a finance textbook, you can value a stock based on earnings or dividends, but sometimes stocks that have neither are the most valuable of all. Tesla has sold a lot of cars, but has not made a lot of money—and it is one of the most expensive stocks out there. I mean, I've been involved in the markets for 24 years, and I don't have the answer to this. It's always seemed to me that the best-performing stocks are the ones that inspire *dreams* in investors. Sometimes those dreams are realized, and sometimes they aren't.

I mentioned dividends—some stocks pay dividends, which is where the company takes a portion of its earnings and pays it out to shareholders on a per-share basis. I am a big fan of stocks with dividends, and I am a big fan of reinvesting dividends back into the stock. I will give you the secret to all of investing right here: *invest in stocks where the dividends are growing, and reinvest the dividends.* Most brokerage firms give you the option of reinvesting the dividends rather than taking the cash—I highly recommend this. This is how you get that exponential growth over time.

I just have to throw in one educational point here—a lot of people think that if stock ABC is trading at 50 bucks, and stock XYZ is trading at 100 bucks, then stock XYZ is worth more than ABC. That's not necessarily the case. The price of a stock is quite arbitrary—how you value a company is based on the price of the stock times the number of shares outstanding.

So to continue the example, let's say that XYZ has a billion shares outstanding, and ABC has three billion shares outstanding. XYZ is $100 a share times a billion shares, making it worth $100 billion. ABC is $50 a share times three billion shares, making it worth $150 billion. So ABC is a more valuable company than XYZ, even though the stock price is lower. Weird, right? Anyway, you don't need to do all this math; just pull up Yahoo! Finance and look to where it says "market capitalization." That will tell you how much the company is worth.

Trading stocks is fun, but my recommendation is that you don't do it unless you have $100,000 saved up. That's because in order to build a diversified portfolio, you're going to need about 20–30 stocks, and it's pointless to try to do that if you have less money. But most people don't care about building a diversified portfolio. They're just punting stuff around. And there is a place for that, but that's not your retirement money. It's screwing-around money. It's okay to have screwing-around money, but it should be no more than 10% of your net worth. Yes, occasionally you will bet big on a stock and knock it out of the park. Some people did it with Tesla, and it worked out.

Chef does not recommend. If you're trading individual stocks, it should be a hobby, not a plan to get rich. That's a good way to scone yourself.

The better way to build wealth in stocks over time is through mutual funds or ETFs—and I prefer mutual funds. A mutual fund is an investment company that offers shares directly to the public. As a hypothetical example, you send in a $3,000 check to a mutual fund, and you get 14.6895 shares of the fund. The fund doesn't trade on an exchange—if you want to get your money out, you have to send a redemption order and you can sell your shares back to the mutual fund firm on the closing net asset value. Mutual funds have been around for eons, and while they do have their shortcomings, I believe the structure is more conducive to long-term investing than that of ETFs. It's because mutual funds aren't exchange-listed, and don't trade throughout the day, so you're not staring at your phone all day, wondering if you should sell.

This is part of a larger point about the periodicity of information—the less information you get on the price of an asset, the better. That's why your house isn't an investment— though it is often a *great* investment because there's no mark-to-market. On any given day, you don't know what your house is worth—at least, not until Zillow came along. If you don't know the price of something, you can leave it alone, and let it compound and grow over time. If you've got a tech stock (or a cryptocurrency) and you're hawking over it every two minutes on your phone, you're going to panic and sell it, and then you will stop compounding. That's why I like mutual funds better than ETFs—you only get one price point a day, rather than a million. I will add that the average person typically makes much more on their house than they do on their stocks, because they leave the house the hell alone.

ETFs are a bit like mutual funds, but have a structure that

is a bit too complex to explain here. They are *kind of* like mutual funds that trade on an exchange. The difference is that the vast majority of ETFs are *index* funds. An index fund is a fund that tracks an index, like the S&P 500, the Nasdaq 100, the Russell 2000, or something else. This is called *passive* management—nobody at the fund is making any investment decisions; they're just passively tracking the index. The opposite is *active* management, where you have a portfolio manager who is picking stocks. There are a lot of dumb debates about active versus passive management—people like to point out that the portfolio managers who pick stocks oftentimes end up underperforming the index. This is true. It also obscures the fact that some actively managed portfolios will have better risk/return characteristics than an index fund. You shouldn't just care about returns—you should also care about risk.

WHAT IS A BOND?

One thing I've learned in my travels is that people really only know about stocks. They know they should invest in bonds, but they don't know why, and they don't know what bonds are.

I was the same way when I started investing—I was reading all these investment books that told me that bonds go up when interest rates go down, so I should invest in bonds for diversification purposes. It made no sense, but I did it anyway. It wasn't until I went to business school and took a class on bond mathematics that I understood why.

The bond math is probably over most people's heads, so we won't do it here, but I'll try to bring it down to eye level.

A bond is a loan. That's all it is. It's a special kind of loan that is traded in the capital markets. This is how it works:

Company XYZ sells a $1,000 bond. They are borrowing $1,000. So they get $1,000 today, and they have to make interest payments every year until the bond matures, and then at maturity they pay back the $1,000 as well.

Let's say interest rates are 5% and it's a five-year bond. So these are the cash flows:

$$-\$1,000 + \$50 + \$50 + \$50 + \$50 + \$1,050$$

The company gets $1,000 today, then pays $50 every year for five years, and on the fifth year, they pay off the principal and the coupon together. That's a bond. The 5% is the *coupon* of the bond—literally the cash that it spits out—but not necessarily the interest rate of the bond. From there, things get a bit more complex.

If you want to know why bond prices go up when interest rates go down, think of it this way—when *market* interest rates go down, say, to 4%, that makes a 5% coupon bond more valuable—so the price goes up.

In practice, you're not going to own individual bonds. You're going to own a bond mutual fund, with lots of individual bonds inside it.

Now, there are all different kinds of bonds. The first is a treasury bond, which is issued by the U.S. government. Treasury bonds are assumed to have zero default risk—you will get paid back. You might get paid back in depreciated currency, but you will get paid back. Treasury bonds are important because they are considered to be the risk-free interest rate, and all other interest rates are benchmarked off of treasury bonds. There's a lot of them out there—$30 trillion in fact, the amount of the U.S.'s debt—so it's a big, liquid market.

Then you have corporate bonds, which are bonds issued by private corporations. They have higher interest rates than treasury bonds, because any corporation—even Walmart—is more likely to default than Uncle Sam. Companies have credit ratings, just like you and I do, which affects their borrowing costs. *Investment-grade* companies have lower interest rates, and *high-yield* companies have higher interest rates. You've probably heard of high-yield bonds before—they're also called junk bonds. Investment-grade corporate bonds are typically pretty boring—junk bonds can get exciting sometimes. Still, a junk bond mutual fund is typically going to be less risky than most stock mutual funds. Again, you won't be buying individual corporate bonds—you'll be buying corporate bond mutual funds.

You also have municipal bonds—these are issued by state and local governments. The key feature of municipal bonds is that the interest is exempt from tax, which makes them appealing to people who have high tax rates—typically rich people. Some rich people will buy individual bonds, but again, it's best to invest in a fund. It makes no sense to invest in municipal bonds if you have a low tax rate, and it makes zero sense to do it in an IRA or 401(k). The municipal bond market is quite large, with tens of thousands of different bonds, and for the vast majority of these bonds, there is no research on them. Still, they *rarely* default. Back in 2009 there was a moral panic about the indebtedness of state and local governments, but it amounted to nothing.

Corporate and municipal bonds are usually rated by credit rating agencies, like Standard & Poor's and Moody's. These rating agencies will examine the financial statements of a company or do some magic math on a municipality and determine the creditworthiness of the issuer. An AAA rating is the highest. Then there is an AA, A, and BBB rating. Those are all *investment grade*. Below that is BB, B, CCC, CC, and D for defaulted. Those bonds are all *high yield*, or junk bonds. C-rated bonds are highly speculative. The worse the rating, the higher the interest rates, but the more likely it is that the company will default. The thing about corporate bonds is that they typically all default at the same time, during a recession. Default rates skyrocketed in 2002 and 2009, and so did interest rates. There were some amazing opportunities then, as yields on high-yield bond funds got well over double digits, but this came with high risk.

There are other bonds that you should know about. There are international government bonds—government bonds issued by foreign governments. There are international corporate bonds as well. And there are convertible bonds—bonds that convert into stock if the stock price goes high enough.

Perhaps your only exposure to bonds has been through *The Big Short*. That movie talked about CDOs—collateralized debt obligations—which is a bunch of bonds sliced and diced and put into tranches, each with their own level of risk.

Back in the 2000s, CDOs were comprised of subprime mortgage bonds that were allocated in this way, with the highest tranche being rated AAA. The movie leads you to believe that there were nefarious motives behind this—there really weren't. The mathematical models that the rating agencies were using didn't account for a coordinated, nationwide drop in housing prices—*because it had never happened.*

Remember, there was a lot of geographic diversity in these CDOs. The AAA tranche of a subprime CDO would only default if all the bonds in the CDO defaulted, which seemed unlikely based on what we knew about the housing market. If you could sum up in a word why the financial system collapsed in 2008, the word would be *correlation*. We did not properly estimate for it. Anyway, this gets back to our earlier discussions on debt. If people buy stocks and they go down, it is generally no big deal. But you can really ruin your life with debt.

I explained a little bit about mortgage bonds, otherwise known as MBS, in an earlier chapter. If you take out a mortgage from a bank, chances are it is going to end up in a pool of mortgages known as an MBS. MBS have their own unique characteristics that are a little too complex to go into here. But you can invest in them—there are mutual funds and ETFs that hold mortgage bonds. They get a little extra yield relative to treasuries, but generally speaking, unlike treasury bonds where you are rooting for interest rates to go down, with mortgage bonds you are rooting for rates to *stay still*.

CURRENCIES

It's possible to invest in foreign currencies, but ordinary people don't generally do this. The U.S. dollar is the biggest by far, followed by the euro, followed by the Japanese yen. There are a bunch of theories on currency valuation, but by and large currency movements follow changes in interest rates. If a country raises interest rates, the currency generally appreciates. That's because you can exchange your home currency into the foreign currency, deposit it in a bank, and earn a higher interest rate. I would say that interest rate differentials explain about 80% of currency movements.

Short-term traders like to trade foreign exchange because FX brokers can offer huge amounts of leverage. A good way to increase your financial stress. Plus, the layperson has no idea what they are doing and so you should avoid it.

COMMODITIES

You can also trade commodities. Here I will disclose that I trade lots of commodities. Examples of commodities include oil, corn, wheat, soybeans, gold, silver, cotton, cocoa, and sugar. In the old days, you had to trade commodities with futures, but now there are ETFs on all the major commodities. Aside from the ETF market, the commodities market remains mostly institutional, because trading futures is a big barrier to entry for a lot of people.

What is a future? It is an agreement to buy or sell something at some day in the future. It is a *derivative*, which is a contract whose price is based on the value of some underlying stock, bond, or commodity. Futures are actually pretty straightforward, but again, futures involve a lot of leverage, and leverage is hazardous to your health. The learning curve is pretty steep. Futures markets provide price discovery for all sorts of commodities that we consume on a daily basis, like wheat, copper, and hogs.

OPTIONS

And you have probably heard about options, too—I wouldn't even bring this up except for the explosion in retail options activity in recent years. Everyone is an options expert these days. No, no you aren't. Options are fiendishly mathematically complex, and I don't recommend trading them unless you have an undergraduate degree in math. And if you are trading options, you are trading with people (and robots) who are far more sophisticated than you. If you want to learn about options, there are other books for that. Billions upon billions were lost by retail investors trading options on GameStop. Billions. They had no idea what they were doing. Long story.

SIMPLE, BORING, DIVERSIFIED

Now that I've introduced you to all this complexity, I want you to ignore it. You'll be building a diversified portfolio of mutual funds and ETFs. Your portfolio should be:

1. Simple
2. Boring
3. Diversified (across asset classes)

The awesome portfolio.

Set it and forget it. Don't look at it. Make regular contributions. Keep adding to it, and pick up your bag of money in 40 years. No stress. Life is good.

The alternative is that you chop yourself to bits trading stocks, currencies, and options for the next 40 years, trying to beat the market. I'm not saying you'll be a failure—I'm saying that the best-case scenario is that you'll be *average*, and it will be a huge amount of work, heartache, and stress. As we've established, stress is what we are trying to avoid.

With that goal in mind, let's look at the awesome portfolio—which really is a silver bullet for your investing career.

....

CHAPTER 14

The Awesome
Portfolio

I have always been on a mission to find the perfect portfolio—
the portfolio that you really could set and forget, and leave
alone for your entire investing lifetime.

That would seem to go against the law of nonstationarity—
the market is a game where the rules constantly change.

But what if there really is a silver bullet? What if there really
is a one-size-fits-all investing solution?

Searching for
the perfect portfolio

The financial industry seems to think that it has a perfect solution already, in the 60/40 portfolio. The 60/40 portfolio is 60% stocks, and 40% bonds. Financial advisors put people into the 60/40 portfolio without really thinking about it, because it is what they have always done. The principle is that when stocks go down, bonds usually go up, and vice versa, which smooths out some of the volatility in the portfolio and leaves everyone happy in the end.

But it doesn't work that way.

The reality is that bonds don't always go up when stocks go down. About half the time, they don't. And they really didn't in 2022, which was a terrible year for stocks, and the worst year for bonds since 1788. The 60/40 portfolio completely sucked in 2022. Stock/bond diversification offered no benefits whatsoever.

And yes, people keep getting funneled into the 60/40 portfolio. The definition of insanity is doing the same thing over again and expecting different results.

The thing with the 60/40 portfolio is that stocks and bonds are both *financial assets*. They are both securities. They are both claims on some future cash flow. But there are different kinds of assets out there, too. There are what is known as *hard assets*. Land, real estate, and commodities. You can invest in these things, too.

Many of us invest in real estate, whether we realize it or not. We buy a house and live in it. It is really an investment in real estate. It is a nondiversified investment in real estate in a specific geographic area, but it is still an investment in real estate. So if you own a house, you invest in real estate. It is a hard asset. Hard assets generally protect against inflation. Real estate usually appreciates in value when inflation goes up. It did this in 2021 and 2022.

But not many of us invest in commodities. In the past, to invest in commodities, you needed the ability to trade futures. But in the last ten years several ETFs have been created to allow individual investors to invest in individual commodities, or baskets of them.

Investing in commodities involves costs to maintain a position, otherwise known as *negative carry*. If you're going to own corn, you have to pay to store the corn. Or oil. Or live cattle. So there is a cost to hold these positions for a long period of time, and it is not small. Depending on the commodity, you might lose 0–8% of the value of your holdings each year because of storage/carry costs. I should add that if you buy commodities through an ETF, the carry costs are passed along to you, the investor. You cannot avoid it.

It makes sense to own stocks because stocks go up over time. But commodities generally don't. In fact, commodities generally go *down* over time as technology improves. Better farming techniques have increased crop yields while decreasing acreage, resulting in lower prices for corn, wheat, and soybeans. Fracking and horizontal drilling kept the price of oil low. If you own commodities, it is essentially a bet against human ingenuity. You are betting that we will mess things up. And there are periods of time where human beings mess things up. But it is not a good long-term bet. Nonetheless, commodities offer *diversification* against stocks and bonds, because they are hard assets, not financial assets. Same thing with real estate.

So if you are going to construct an optimal portfolio, it must have a mix of financial assets and hard assets. I started experimenting with this in 2019. And one thing I discovered was that gold was actually a better diversifier than a basket of commodities. It performed better, too.

The thing about gold is that while it may not be the best asset, it is the asset that has the best contribution to portfolio risk.

Let me put it another way—it is like adding Dennis Rodman to a basketball team. Dennis Rodman isn't so great at scoring, but he is really good at rebounding and passing the ball to his teammates. When you add Dennis Rodman to a team, you make it better. That's why gold works in portfolios. It is the great diversifier. And it also goes up occasionally.

So a good portfolio would own stocks, bonds, real estate, and gold. What else should it own?

It should own *cash*.

Earlier in this book we talked about the benefits of holding cash. Cash has a volatility of zero, so by adding cash to a portfolio, you automatically reduce its volatility. Cash had a return of zero for many years, but now it pays interest again. And cash is also an option to buy things in the future.

There really isn't any good accumulated wisdom out there on the ideal level of cash for a portfolio. Most financial advisors like to keep it as low as possible, so their clients can be *fully invested*, and the more they invest, the more fees they get. People like to be fully invested so they don't "miss out" on market moves. Of course, by being fully invested they don't miss out on bear markets, either.

So the ideal portfolio should have stocks, bonds, cash, gold, and real estate.

In what proportions?

Well, why not keep it simple and give 20% to each?

- 20% stocks
- 20% bonds

- 20% cash
- 20% gold
- 20% real estate

This is what I call the *Awesome Portfolio*.

Back when I had a radio show, I used to call it the 20/20/20/20/20 portfolio, but that was kind of a mouthful, so I said, why not call it the Awesome Portfolio, because it is Awesome!

Let me tell you how awesome it is.

This portfolio is awesome!

I backtested this portfolio back to 1971—the furthest I could go back, because 1971 is when Nixon took the U.S. off the gold standard.

Since 1971, the Awesome Portfolio has returned 8.1% annually, with nearly half the volatility of a portfolio that is 80% stocks and 20% bonds. 8.1% is pretty good—that's not much less than what you might get with just stocks, but with half the volatility.

And this is the key point—up until 2022, the maximum drawdown (max loss) of the Awesome Portfolio in any given year was 9.2%, in 2008. In the Great Financial Crisis, the Awesome Portfolio lost 9.2%. That is a pretty good outcome, when you consider that the S&P 500 experienced a loss of 57% from the peak in 2007 to the low in 2009. In 2022, during a period of sharply rising interest rates—really the Awesome Portfolio's only weakness—it lost 12.1%, whereas stocks lost 19.4% that year.

I'll tell you why this is important. The most important thing about investing is to *stay invested*, so you can keep compounding. Once you panic and sell your stocks and bonds, you stop compounding, and the growth ends. It is of crucial importance to devise a portfolio that you can live with in good times and bad.

Lots of people have a portfolio of all stocks. Like the index fund people. They buy an S&P 500 index fund which perfectly mimics the S&P 500 index. If you invest in an index, you get the returns of the index, which is very good; but you also get the volatility of the index, which is bad. If you invest in the stock market, as represented by a broad market index fund, you will experience all the volatility of the stock market—the ups and downs, the highs and lows. And so will your emotions. You will be elated on the all-time highs, and demoralized on the all-time lows.

The nice thing about the Awesome Portfolio is that it gives you some exposure to things that benefit from inflation—like real estate and gold. At the time of writing, we're currently experiencing some inflation, and I think it will persist for some time. In theory, stocks benefit from inflation, too, or at a minimum, pass it along. Bonds do not benefit from inflation at all.

Remember, I said earlier that the ideal investment would be a CD or savings account that spits out 8% a year, and grows in a straight-line fashion. The Awesome Portfolio isn't that, but it is about as close as you can get—8% a year with minimum volatility.

This is where I insert the disclaimer that past performance is no indication of future results, but the past performance is pretty dang good. It works because it has the best risk/reward characteristics of any portfolio. It allows you to *stay invested*.

If the worst year you can possibly have is down 12.1%, there is a good chance that you won't panic out of your portfolio. You can stay invested, and keep compounding.

I can't tell you how many stories I've heard over the years of people who panicked out of their stocks at the ding-dong lows, and completely missed out on the bull market that followed. It happens in every single cycle.

Now, there is a cohort of index fund adherents that say you should just buy and hold, ride out the volatility, and dollar-cost average along the way. Very few people can do that in a bear market as severe as the 2007–08 financial crisis. I do know one person that did, and he ended up doing very well. But only one. That takes a hardy constitution. I'm not much in the mood to sit back and watch my net worth drop 57%. Let me put it this way—even if I *could* ride it out, it would be so awful that I'd be miserable to be around for a period of a couple of years.

Remember, this whole gig is about living a stress-free financial life, but what the index fund adherents want you to do is to live a life that is full of financial stress, riding the ups and downs of every bull and bear market. It isn't necessary. With the Awesome Portfolio, you trade about a percentage point in performance for a whole lot less risk. You can sleep soundly at night, which is what counts.

It seems as though people want to do the things that *maximize* their financial stress. Index funds are just the tip of the iceberg. People buy growth stocks, SPACs, or crypto. They're always looking for the new, new thing. They spend too much time on Twitter or Reddit. They buy options like a degenerate. People need action. They need that *fix*.

Let me just tell you that I don't have much of a taste for gambling. Sure, I'll gamble—I'll walk up to a $25 craps table with about $500, play the pass line for about 45 minutes, and if I lose a few hundred bucks, I'll stop myself out and quit. Or I might put $200 on a baseball game in the sports book. That's about the extent of it. I've gone to casinos and *not* gambled. I go shopping instead. Even when I worked at Lehman Brothers, I really had to work to increase my risk appetite. It does not come naturally to me.

My advice to you is: if you like to gamble, carve out about 10% of your money that you will use to speculate, and leave the other 90% in the Awesome Portfolio. There is nothing wrong with a little recreational punting around. Like I said before, investing is a hobby, and it's a fun hobby, and people put a lot of effort into it. But the sad reality is that you are probably not as good as you think you are, and if you speculate with your retirement savings, there will probably be a sad ending. Maybe you do think you are that good. Maybe you have had a run of good luck. It is probably luck, and you will revert to the mean at some point. Again: it's a hobby. Go to work and be a W-2 employee and earn a paycheck and keep that income stream coming in. It's the most powerful personal finance thing you can do.

Maybe you are wondering about this 8% return that the Awesome Portfolio offers. Maybe you think those returns are a little skinny. Actually, they are pretty good. For sure, you could earn 9% in a broad-based index fund—*if* you can hang on. You get to earn an extra 1% if you can manage to ride out the volatility.

If you invest in the Awesome Portfolio, you can go on about your day, playing golf or petting cats or whatever you do with your spare time, *not thinking about your investments*—maybe checking on them once per year. And at the end, you'll have more than enough for retirement.

Implementation

Let's talk about implementation. Remember I said I like mutual funds better than ETFs. The Awesome Portfolio is much easier to implement with ETFs. If this all sounds complicated, it's not—it's easy.

We're going to build the portfolio using five ETFs.

Let me explain this, step by step.

20% stocks: The best ETF here is VTI—the Vanguard Total Stock Market Index Fund. You might be tempted to use an S&P 500 index fund. I suggest you don't—you want the small-cap stocks, too. And the Vanguard funds have the lowest fees.

20% bonds: BND—the Vanguard Total Bond Market Index Fund. There are others like it, but this has the lowest fees. This ETF has all kinds of bonds—treasury, corporate, mortgage, and more, across maturities. It is the best representation of the U.S. bond market.

20% cash: Here, I recommend a money market mutual fund. Any will do—there isn't much difference between them. There are prime money market funds and treasury money market funds. The treasury money market funds just have T-bills—the prime funds have commercial paper and other instruments. The prime money market funds have a tiny amount of credit risk, and they have a slightly higher yield. Either is fine.

20% gold: Here you want to use the ETF GLD, or SPDR Gold Trust. GLD has been around since 2005—each share is worth (approximately) a tenth of an ounce of gold. The shares of the ETF are backed by actual physical gold in a vault in London. It's the easiest and most convenient way to own gold. You hold it in your brokerage account just like any other stock.

20% real estate: This will take some explanation. If you own real estate, you would consider the *equity* in your house as part of your real estate allocation. If you own a $300,000 house and you have 25% equity, then you have $75,000 in equity, and you would use that as your real estate allocation. If you don't own a house, then the best way to get exposure is through the ETF VNQ—the Vanguard REIT Index. A REIT is a real estate investment trust—a company that passively invests in various real estate, and VNQ is a basket of a bunch of REITs. It's a good way to get exposure to the real estate sector. For a lot of people, when considering the equity in their house, they will probably have *too big* of a real estate exposure relative to the rest of the Awesome Portfolio. That's fine—you can work on adding to the other asset classes over time. If you have too small of a real estate exposure through your house, you can add some REITs to bring you up to 20%.

And that's it. Pretty simple.

Fully embrace the awesome

I have been writing about the Awesome Portfolio for a few years, and my experience with this is that people think it is cool, and they carve out about a 10–20% slice of their brokerage account for it. That's nice, but that kind of misses the point.

The point is that you'll put *all* of your money in the Awesome Portfolio, except for maybe a 10% tranche of screwing-around money for your investing hobby.

I don't want to be the financial guru that recommends a strategy to the general public, only to have it blow up. But I'm pretty sure it's not going to blow up. I've stress-tested this a million different ways, and the only vulnerability I've detected is rising interest rates, which led to the Awesome Portfolio's subpar performance in 2022. There could be a black swan— maybe the government confiscates gold again, like it did in the 1930s. Outside of something unforeseen like that, I think the Awesome Portfolio is as safe as it gets. Certainly safer than the U.S. stock market, which has had four great bear markets of 50% or more. The Awesome Portfolio has bonds—lots of people think that bonds are safe. The Awesome Portfolio has cash—pretty much everyone thinks that cash is safe. People think that gold is safe. The likelihood that it all goes pear-shaped at the same time is negligible. Trust me—I probably think about risk and safety more than you do.

Monitoring

I should mention one thing about the Awesome Portfolio: you do need to pay a tiny bit of attention to it. You must *rebalance* it once per year.

What does that mean?

Well, in any given year, stocks may go up, bonds may go down, gold may go sideways, and real estate may go down, and your weightings will no longer be 20%.

Once per year, whenever you want (it is arbitrary), you must sell the stuff that is up and buy the stuff that is down and return it to something approximating 20% weights across the board. You shouldn't do this every month or every quarter—you should do this once per year, exactly, on the same date every year (there are mathematical reasons why you should do this which are too complex for this book). Put a reminder in your phone. You will have to do some back-of-the-envelope math.

Correspondingly, as you earn income and you want to invest in the Awesome Portfolio periodically, I suggest making contributions proportionally across asset classes. You might find this to be a nuisance, but I assure that it is important to maintain the appropriate weights. Having said that, you don't need to get too scientific about it—it doesn't have to be correct down to the penny. Close enough for government work.

One last thing I want to cover—the temptation to fiddle with the Awesome Portfolio can be irresistible. For example, the recommended stock allocation is VTI—the Vanguard Total Stock Market Index fund. I'm sure there are some people saying out there—why not put it in small cap stocks? Small caps have outperformed over time. Why not put it in midcap? Why not put it in value? Why not include some international stocks? There are a million ways you can muck with this.

Look. I'm not one of those annoying purists. The important thing is that 20% of your portfolio is allocated to stocks. If you want to try to game the system by doing style box trades, that's up to you, but if you have any experience investing, you know there can be some massive differences in performance between large and small-cap, growth and value, and U.S. and international. If you get it wrong, the Awesome Portfolio won't work. And then you will blame me, the Awesome Portfolio guy. I can tell you that it will work if you buy *all U.S. stocks.*

There are other ways to change it up, too. You can buy corporate bonds or high-yield bonds instead of *all* bonds. You can buy gold miners instead of actual gold. You can get cute about real estate.

I implore you not to get cute. Sure, it may work out—but it may not. What you're essentially doing is being an active manager—and we know how well active managers do against the index. If you passively track the Awesome Index, there is a good chance that you will get something approximating those historical returns.

Don't try to be too smart about it. You only have to look at this portfolio once per year, when you rebalance. When you do rebalance, you might be tempted to allocate more to stocks, gold, etc., if they are performing well. Nope. Go back to the 20% weights, which will also require you to buy more of the things that are underperforming. It takes a tiny amount of discipline. It does take a little bit of patience. There will be stretches of a few years where the Awesome Portfolio doesn't do much of anything. You might get bored with it. Please, wait for the poison to take effect.

Correlation

One thing you will notice about the Awesome Portfolio if you observe it over time is that it's pretty rare that *everything* is working at once. Stocks and bonds will be up, but gold will be down. Real estate will be up, but bonds will be down. That's by design.

I want to introduce you to the term *correlation*, which is the property that two different asset class move together, like a marching band. Stocks, you will notice, move like a marching band. If the Dow is up 1,000 points, nearly all stocks will be up. They are correlated. The same is true within the bond market. But once you start diversifying across *asset classes*, the correlation breaks down. If you add uncorrelated assets to a portfolio, it reduces the volatility—which is the goal.

Remember, volatility is the enemy; the purpose of volatility is to make people make stupid decisions. Volatility is also the enemy of your lizard brain. It stresses you out, and makes you feel anxious. The Awesome Portfolio, in any given year, or multiple years, can and will lose money. But not a lot. 2022 was the worst year for the Awesome Portfolio—ever—and it still wasn't that bad.

The future
of investing?

The Awesome Portfolio is such an important innovation—and my hope is that someday it will be adopted by the investment advisory industry. That will take some doing. Banks and brokers have been shoving people into 60/40 portfolios for years, with execrable results. One thing that is true about the financial industry is that you can't get fired for losing money as long as you're doing what everyone else is doing. If you put someone in a 60/40 portfolio and they lose 20%, nobody loses their job—"It's just what everyone does." There's so much careerism and conformism it's not even funny. Even my own financial advisor, who loves the Awesome Portfolio, still puts people into 60/40 model portfolios that his firm creates. That is what they are compensated on. It's pervasive, and it's dangerous, and 2022 was an example of how bad it can be. But I think the industry is ripe for change. In 2022, there was a lot of chatter about "the end of the 60/40 portfolio." Nobody has an answer for what will replace it—but I do.

My guess is if you read this book and you photocopy this chapter on the Awesome Portfolio and hand it to your advisor, and tell him or her that is how you want to invest, they will refuse. They will not take the risk. They won't understand the math behind it, they won't bother to look at the historical returns, and they'll dismiss it as the rantings of some crank author with another get-rich-quick scheme. Also, they won't be getting any commissions on those fee-based mutual funds that they typically offer. But generally, financial advisors will do what their clients tell them to do, so if you persist, they will acquiesce. And then you'll never need to buy another mutual fund again.

This is also a good way not to pay a lot of fees. If you buy one of those mutual funds offered by your financial advisor, you will pay something like a 3% front-end load and some ongoing expenses. If you invest in the Awesome Portfolio, you will pay some commissions on the way in and a small amount of commissions to rebalance. The fees should be a fraction of what they would be with a full-service investment advisor. And you can do it yourself.

I worked on Wall Street for 20 years before I came up with this innovation. I needed every single day of investment experience. This is the solution. Every single financial advisor in America should be putting their clients into the Awesome Portfolio. Think of the heartache it would save. Think of how it would eliminate the need for those hard conversations. Maybe it would even eliminate the need for financial advisors.

I think have arrived at the answer.

PART V

....

Relief

CHAPTER 15

·······································

Stability

The two extremes

I have met a lot of people over the years, and studied their financial behavior. I have met some incredible CFs and some incredible high rollers. And you know what the funny thing about these people is? *They think they have all the answers, that they are the experts at managing money, and that everyone else is wrong.*

The funny thing about this is that people are generally hard-wired to become CFs or high rollers, but they believe that they arrived at these conclusions on their own, intellectually speaking. They have a *philosophy* of money. They either have a scarcity philosophy—*money is hard to get*—or an abundance philosophy—*money is easy to get*. And that drives all of their behavior.

Over the years, I have met CFs who:

- Get the cheapest thing on the menu, wherever they go.
- Harass contractors and vendors for discounts and free stuff.
- Buy things on credit cards, and get refunds on debit cards, so they can keep the points.
- Tip $1 on a $50 check.
- Haggle over price on every single item they buy.
- Refuse to send their kids to private school, even when they have the means to do it, and the public schools are terrible.
- Keep inordinate amounts of money in a checking or savings account, for safety.
- Return their kids' birthday presents, for cash.
- Stay in the cheapest hotels possible when traveling on vacation.
- Have "alligator arms," and never be the one to pick up the bill.
- Eat 69 cent cans of pork and beans for lunch.
- Buy generic brand everything at the grocery store.
- Have never bought a new car in their life.
- Have millions in savings and choose to live in a lower-middle-class neighborhood.
- Crash on people's couches instead of paying for a hotel.
- Make their kids pay for their own college education, when there is plenty of money available.
- Never donate to charity.
- Buy short-term investment-grade corporate bonds (and nothing else).

Now, there is a good chance that you're reading this list, and you *identified* with it. You're like, "Yeah, that's the answer. Whoever this guy is, he's doing it right."

Let me assure you that this guy is not doing it right. I will explain why.

Someone who goes to these measures to save money is spending a lot of time *thinking about money*. They're doing all the mental mathematics on how much they save by getting a muffin instead of a chicken biscuit and multiplying that by 250 days a year and calculating how much they'll be able to put in their retirement account, and watching it compound at 8% over 40 years. They're doing all that math with every purchase they make. They are spending a lot of time *thinking about money*. It is an obsession.

I don't know about you, but I don't want to spend any time at all thinking about money. There are a lot better things to think about than money. The night before I wrote this chapter, I went out to dinner with my nephew and his wife. The bill came to $81. I had a brainfart and gave the waitress $120 and didn't ask for any change. I meant to give her $100, but I just did the math wrong in my head. So she got a 50% tip. I felt dumb, but $20 is not going to make or break me, and she probably really appreciated it, so I didn't dwell on it. I certainly am not going to miss a mortgage payment over $20.

I can assure you that the hypothetical person in this example would dwell on this mistake. Or, more likely, they wouldn't have made the mistake in the first place, because they're *that careful* with money. They certainly wouldn't tip someone 50% on purpose, because they see money as a zero-sum game. If you get less, then I get more. Their sole purpose in life is to accumulate as much wealth as possible, one nickel at a time, until the end, and—then what? What was all that effort for? What was the purpose? They work and save, and work and save, and never stop for a moment to enjoy the fruits of their labor. It is nothing but decades of pointless asceticism.

Then, you get people on the opposite end of the spectrum:

- Go to a restaurant and order three times much food as everyone needs.
- A closet full of clothes that they never wear.
- Come across an unexpected windfall and immediately buy an expensive car (and finance it).
- Multiple six figures in credit card debt.
- Negative equity on the house, after multiple cash-out refinancings.
- Income barely covers the debt service.
- Six different gym memberships.
- Twelve different streaming services.
- Dozens of subscriptions.
- Generous to a fault, donating thousands to charity, leaving nothing for the family.
- Obsessed with image—must have the best car, the best clothes, the best house. Everything has to be "the best."
- Has had liquidity problems and borrowed from friends or family.
- Always teetering on the edge of bankruptcy.
- No margin of safety.
- Cash doesn't stay in the bank account for long, before it is spent.
- No savings; no retirement accounts whatsoever.
- Buys dogecoin and GameStop.

There is a good chance that you read through this list and you identified with this, as well. You have an abundance mentality. There is no problem with spending money, because you will always make more. You are an optimist. You always believe that you have the ability to make more money. So you are generous with friends, with family members, and with charities. You like to show off. You like to show off how *rich* you are—it is important that you are *seen* buying five times as much as you need *of anything*. Even a quick trip to the grocery store is a $500 affair.

The difference between these two hypothetical people is that the personal finance industry sees the first person as an example to uphold, and the second person as an example of all that is wrong with the U.S.—big spenders and debt slaves. The reality is that the first example is much more common than the second example, and a lot of that is because of the efforts of the personal finance folks, who have demonized the person in the second example as reckless and irresponsible.

The truth is that they are *both bad*—because neither of these people has a *healthy relationship with money*. A healthy relationship with money is where you don't spend any time thinking about money. Both of these people spend a lot of time thinking about money. In the first example, how to scrounge up more and save it; and in the second example, how to stay ahead of the monthly payments. The truth, as always, is somewhere in between.

It is true that money is meant to be enjoyed, and that if you spend four decades living like a monk, you would have failed in this respect. But some people enjoy money a little too much—and then have to worry about how they are going to pay for all the stuff they bought. In both cases, these people can damage relationships. In the first example, by being a CF, and doing things like not paying for college. In the second example, when it all comes crashing down (which it inevitably will). If you're managing your financial affairs in such a way that it will hurt the people around you, when the consequences of your actions extend to family members and beyond, then you should rethink what you are doing.

This requires restoring some *balance* to your life.

Restoring balance

You see, the thing is that it's easy to preach extreme solutions. The personal finance gurus have been preaching extreme solutions for decades. On one hand, live in a 1,200-square foot house, buy a 20-year-old car, eat ramen noodles. On the other hand, go into as much debt as possible, buy houses and laundromats, and live off the passive income. I just described two of the most popular personal finance books of all time. There is nothing in between: just be a normal human being and have a healthy relationship with money. Money is a tool, and if you let it dominate or control you, you lose.

I would guess about 50% of people fall into the first category (CF) and 30% of people fall into the second category (high roller). Only about 20% of people have a healthy relationship with money. If this describes you—if you didn't identify with either of these fictitious examples—congratulations. I hope you got something out of this book nonetheless.

If you find yourself cutting uncanceled stamps off of envelopes, or buying 11 sandwiches for three people, then you are in the extreme zone. You are not in the middle.

I have a strong personal dislike of the term "everything in moderation" because there are examples when extreme solutions are preferable. Alcoholics, for example, must pursue a course of abstinence. For food addicts and sex addicts, on the other hand, abstinence is nearly impossible, so some guardrails must be put in place. The same is true with spending. You can't *not* spend money and participate in civilized society. So you must necessarily pursue a course of moderation—*which is the hardest thing to do in the world.*

What is the "right" amount of spending? How do you know what is the right amount? Well, a good guideline is that you occasionally buy things that make you happy and you do it without the use of debt, and there is plenty left over for savings. That is pretty much it.

On the investment side, moderation means that you have to take a little bit of risk. What is the right amount of risk? Well, if you find yourself checking your phone to look at your dogecoin or AMC positions every five minutes, you are probably taking too much risk. If you are looking at any of your investments more than once a day, you are probably taking too much risk. If you have all your money in the bank, you are not taking enough risk.

I have mentioned before that at one point in my career, I took too much risk. It was a nightmare that lasted about three years. I really, really do not want to go through that ever again. Some people spend their entire lives like that, in a state of heightened arousal, waiting for infinity or zero. And some people are exceptionally risk-averse, and spend an inordinate amount of time thinking of ways things can go wrong. A third way is to take a medium amount of risk, in an intelligent fashion, and then go on and live your life, *not thinking about money*.

How about debt? Some people hate debt—and never use it if at all possible. Some people love debt, and in a perverse way, the extreme amount of debt motivates them to work harder. By this point, you've read my thoughts on debt, and you know that I am not much of a fan. Still, the vast majority of people in the U.S. will get a mortgage to buy a house—and it wouldn't have been possible unless they had. Debt can help you achieve your financial goals, if used responsibly and judiciously. Some people get a little carried away. A lot of people attach moral significance to debt—in some cultures, it is forbidden entirely, along with the charging of interest.

Here is how debt works: there is something you want to buy, but you don't have the money, so you borrow the money if and when you have ample income to support the payments. It's that simple. We have very sophisticated ways of figuring out if people have too much debt: credit scores. If you can't get your credit score above 700, chances are you have too much debt.

You want to have the right amount of debt and the right amount of risk—which is a lot harder than *no* debt or *no* risk— it's a judgement call. That's why extreme solutions sell so well. "Cut up your credit cards and live off the grid" is a lot easier to implement than "Take a little bit of debt—but not too much. Take a little bit of risk—but not too much." Very difficult to do.

Some people think that if you have no debt and no risk, then you do not have financial stress. Nothing could be further from the truth. The first type of person that I described, the type of person with no debt and no risk, spends a lot of time thinking about money. How to get it, how to keep it, how to hang onto it. They are consumed with these thoughts on a daily basis. The person with lots of debt and lots of risk is also consumed with thoughts about money on a daily basis—how do I stay ahead of the repo man. The person in the middle, who practices broad acceptance with their financial affairs, is the most at peace. Your relationship with money is not too different than your relationship with other things. If you eat too much, you are obese. If you don't eat enough, you are anorexic. You want to have a healthy relationship with food. Money is no different.

It's not that I don't worry about things. I worry about plenty of things. My anxiety is probably higher than the average person. I worry about the cats. I worry about my house being built. I worry about my job. I really worry about my relationships with other people. But I don't worry about money—ever. Money is the dumbest thing in the world to worry about.

This is the point in the discussion at which someone asks me: "What about the person that doesn't have any?" Two things: first, I have met plenty of people who don't have any money who are perfectly happy. And second, that situation is relatively easy to resolve. Even in the worst job markets in the U.S., someone who wants a job can usually get one. There are always ways to scramble and make money. Getting it is relatively straightforward—it's what you do with it once you have it that's the problem.

What I want for you

I want you to get to the point where you can go out to dinner with three people and pick up the tab, as an act of pure generosity—not because you are trying to show off. The first type of person will have the alligator arms—and will ask for separate checks. The second type of person will insist on buying, making a big show of it.

If you are one of these people who goes out to dinner and the check comes and it causes you *anxiety*, then you do not have a healthy relationship with money. If you are one of these people who goes out to dinner and the check comes, and you're running through this mental inventory of what everyone ate and drank, and how much they should owe, you do not have a healthy relationship with money.

Someone with a healthy relationship with money just doesn't worry about any of this. Someone with a healthy relationship with money doesn't say to themselves, "Well, *he* didn't pay the last two times, so *he* should pay this time"—trust me, you are the only person that cares about things like this. And if someone really is a cheapskate, it will catch up with them eventually—word will get around. I believe strongly in financial karma.

I want you to get to the point where you can pay for your child's college education—and do it with grace and dignity, without having to remind the family every third day about all the money you're forking over to Cheesesteak U. Or pay for a vacation without bringing up the fact that it came out of your pocket. Balance is about going through life gracefully, and not getting into fights about money. Fights about money are the worst fights of all, because that $50 you're fighting about just does not matter. At all. And relationships are ended over less than $50. People say, "Well, it's the principle of the thing." No, just suck it up, and decide if you want to continue the relationship. I have ended friendships, but never about money, and I have some friends that are the cheapest of CFs.

I want to you to be able to live *at* your means. Not above your means, or below your means, but at your means. I have a friend who is an investment banker who makes multiple millions per year. As of a few years ago, he was still buying his suits at Jos. A. Bank. He was advanced enough in his career that he would occasionally be socializing with politicians and celebrities. I said, "Dude, you might want to spend a little more money on the suits. People notice—and they care." He replied to me forcefully: "No one notices, and no one cares." He eventually graduated to some custom suits that were still relatively inexpensive.

Someone who makes $3 million a year should be spending $1,500 on a suit—at a minimum. Someone who makes $100,000 a year can buy the $350 suit from Men's Wearhouse. Someone who is a millionaire has a duty to spend more money—or else be labeled a cheapskate. Conversely, someone who makes $80,000 a year who spends $1,500 on a suit has misplaced priorities—or they care very deeply about their personal appearance.

If you're a millionaire, not only *can* you buy the $80,000 car, you *should* buy the $80,000 car. Trust me—you will enjoy it. A lot better than buying an eight-year-old Chrysler Sebring that smells like cigarette smoke and the electronics don't work. Those are the types of things you do when you are first starting out—not late in your career, when you should be enjoying the fruits of your labor.

I have strong feelings about this. I went through a period of time where I was living below my means. I was working for Lehman Brothers, making almost a million dollars a year, and was living in a small, 1,600-square foot house in West New York, NJ. If you're familiar with West New York, you know there are some luxury houses and apartments down by the river in Port Imperial. I was living up on the cliffs, in a less nice neighborhood. It wasn't great. Now, part of this was because of an investment thesis—I figured it would get gentrified. It never did. I ended up actually losing money on that house. And it was a little embarrassing having people over to visit, when most of my peers were living in Summit or Short Hills, NJ. *Having said that*, when the financial crisis hit, it was good that I didn't have most of my wealth tied up in expensive real estate. But it was a little ludicrous that I was the head of ETF trading for Lehman Brothers and lived in an old, tiny house in a crappy neighborhood. I was living below my means.

From then on, I have been very intent on living *at* my means. Not above my means, but at my means. I spent some money on clothes. I bought an expensive car. I am in the process of building the house. I'm experienced with money, and I know how to do the math around these sorts of things, so I've been very careful every step of the way to make sure I never was overextended. And I've enjoyed a higher standard of living. I have a nice house and a nice car. It gives me pleasure. Remember, I am a former CF. I *denied* myself luxuries up until about age 38, at which point I said, "What am I doing? I can afford this stuff." If you're like me, a CF, the thing you have to remember is that you are not *morally superior* to the high roller. You are creating as much havoc in your life as they are, just in different ways.

I like to think that I maintain a good balance between saving and spending, debt and risk. Occasionally I find myself out of balance, at which point it's good to step back, re-evaluate, and get back in balance. If I find myself thinking too much about money, I know I am out of balance. I don't want to be thinking about money, because money isn't thinking about me.

I want you to be able to make small financial decisions without thinking about them—and think *a lot* about large financial decisions. The price of a can of soup literally does not matter, and you can stop spending five minutes staring at all the cans of soup in the grocery store to find the cheapest one. The price of a house and the interest rate on a mortgage matter a lot, and you should spend a lot of time thinking about negotiating and what type of mortgage you are going to get. It's the big decisions that count, not the little decisions.

If you want to spend an extra $5 a week and get your cat Fancy Feast instead of Friskies, I'm pretty sure you can make it work, and the cat will be happy. If you want to put a pool in your backyard, you should think long and hard about it. But there are a lot of idiots out there who tell you that it is the little things that matter, and if you agonize over all these thousands and millions of financial decisions, you will one day be rich. Well, maybe they are right. But you will be miserable in the process.

....

I'm not in the financial business. Yes, I have spent a long career in finance, but I would not consider myself to be one of the world's top financial minds. I am not in the money business; I am in the happy business. And the key to financial happiness is to get to a place where not only do you not worry about money, but you don't think about it at all.

Thinking back to the movie *The Gambler*, wouldn't it be nice to be operating from a position of f★★★ you. Quit your job anytime you want? Own your house, have a couple bucks in the bank, don't drink. That's your fortress of solitude.

I would love for every reader of this book to one day be operating from that position. You certainly can't be if you're in debt. You can't be if you're taking too much risk. Save judiciously, pay down debt, own assets, and nobody can tell you what to do. Nobody can touch you. You're untouchable. Lose your income—no big deal. Someone gets sick—no big deal. Nothing is a big deal. That's peace—and happiness. A life free from financial worry.

We all want it for ourselves—why not make it happen?

THE END

ACKNOWLEDGEMENTS

....

I want to thank my cats *first*—Stripe, Tars, Uma, Vesper, Wendy, Xenia, and Yellow—for sitting next to me on the couch as I wrote the majority of this book in the fall of 2021.

Then I want to thank my wife, Carolyn, who read the chapters as I wrote them, giving me helpful feedback and encouragement.

I want to thank my editor, Craig Pearce, for fatefully reaching out to me over email to see what I was working on at the end of 2021, and for his superb editing skills, taking all the naughty bits out of the book so we could reach a wider audience. Craig clearly has a lot more maturity than I do.

Thanks also go to my literary agent Stephen Barr for sending the proposal through an eight-month car wash, as it came out much better on the other side.

Most of all, I'd like to thank (now retired) professor James Lough at Savannah College of Art and Design. The proposal for this book was conceived in his class, *The Publishing Process*.

Also thanks to my thesis committee at SCAD: Lee Griffith, Andrea Goto, and Chris Millis for giving me much-needed feedback and making the book better.

I'd like to thank my partners at Jared Dillian Money, Olivier

Garret and Ed D'Agostino, for believing in me and this project, and also for putting me on the radio, where I developed these ideas night after night over the course of two long years.

Finally, I'd like to thank the folks at RealVision for inviting me down to the Cayman Islands in 2022—it was there that I put the finishing touches on the manuscript while sitting on my hotel balcony, listening to the chickens.

And thank *you*, the reader, for making it to the end.